RAILWAY RAMBLES *in* SNOWDONIA

Featuring the
Great Little Trains of Wales!

Ian Coulthard

Published by Sigma Leisure – an imprint of
Sigma Press, 5 Alton Road, Wilmslow, Cheshire SK9 5DY, England.

British Library Cataloguing in Publication Data
A CIP record for this book is available from the British Library.

ISBN: 1 85058 800 7

Typesetting and Design by: Sigma Press, Wilmslow, Cheshire.

Cover photographs: main picture, Llanberis Lake Railway; small pictures, left to right: the Talyllyn, Ffestiniog and Fairbourne railways *(Graham Beech)*

Photographs: All by the author except where indicated; photographs for walks 9 and 19 were provided by the Ffestiniog Railway, the photographers being John Peduzzi and Roger Dimmick.

Maps: by Bute Cartographics, based on 1952 and 1953 Ordnance Survey maps. OS licence number MC100032058.

Printed by: Interprint Ltd, Malta

Disclaimer: the information in this book is given in good faith and is believed to be correct at the time of publication. No responsibility is accepted by either the author or publisher for errors or omissions, or for any loss or injury howsoever caused. Only you can judge your own fitness, competence and experience. Do not rely solely on sketch maps for navigation: we strongly recommend the use of appropriate Ordnance Survey (or equivalent) maps.

Foreword

By Peter Austin, once a long-distance walker and now
Secretary of The Great Little Trains of Wales[*]

As a boy, growing up in south London in the late 1940s, I first had a fascination for the main line engines that rattled past, belching smoke, soot and steam on my daily walk to and from school. Later, work took me to Barry in South Wales, and I witnessed first-hand what must have been the largest steam locomotive graveyard ever. During my leisure time and when not exploring past industrial archaeology, I took to the hills. Inter alia, I have followed Wainwright from Coast to Coast and along the Pennine Way, traversed the Pembrokeshire Coast Path and even walked from Cardiff to Conwy (The Cambrian Way) over most of the well-known peaks of Wales. It was in the late 1960s that I first set foot in Snowdonia, and I have been captivated by the might and magnificence of its scenery ever since – so much so that now, early-retired, I have recently moved to live on its southern perimeter and to work with the Talyllyn Railway.

I know that I am not alone in sharing an interest in both trains and walking, evidenced by the number of railway passengers I regularly see who are so obviously dressed for walking. Imagine my delight, therefore, when I was invited to write a foreword to a book that combines my pastimes. Here, then, for the very first time we have a collection of linear walks where each of the Great Little Trains of Wales is used to transport the walker to or from his expedition; standard-gauge, main line train services are also utilised, sometimes in conjunction with these narrow-gauge steam railways. This book demonstrates how walkers and train enthusiasts can indulge both passions. It contains a wide range of walks to suit everyone; up and down valleys, along coasts and over the hills and mountains of

---

[*] The Great Little Trains of Wales is a marketing consortium of independent, narrow gauge steam railways. Further details, including a timetable pack, can be obtained by writing to: The Secretary, Great Little Trains of Wales, Wharf Station, Tywyn, Gwynedd LL36 9EY – please include your name and contact address!

Wales. An extra dimension is added by walking in the superb scenery of Snowdonia, where the railways are utilised to access more remote routes and quiet, lesser-used footpaths and tracks.

For those on holiday, Great Little Trains of Wales Wanderer tickets can offer savings for regular travellers on any of the preserved railways over a one or two week period. I would commend this book to those with similar interests to myself – who knows, we may even meet when there's steam and smoke in the air, I've whistle and flag in hand or a stick with stout boots on foot!

Peter Austin

Preface

This collection of linear walks based mainly, but not exclusively, in Snowdonia is mainly in the range from a few miles over fairly level ground to energetic walks eleven miles long over mountains, with a height gain of nearly 1500 feet. They all involve taking a train ride on a preserved railway, the standard gauge national network, or a combination of the two. It is also possible to combine two of the shorter walks where the end of one walk and the start of another use the same railway station.

Most of the preserved railways in Snowdonia are in "The Great Little Trains of Wales" marketing group which also includes three lines outside Snowdonia, namely Vale of Rheidol, Welshpool and Llanfair, and Brecon Mountain Railways. Three 'bonus' walks – 28, 29 and 30 – using the latter three railways have, therefore, been included in this book.

The book was inspired by the re-building of the Welsh Highland Railway line between Caernarfon and Porthmadog. This is an extremely ambitious project with many daunting obstacles. The first 11 miles from Caernarfon to Rhyd Ddu, at the foot of Snowdon, opened in the summer of 2003 thanks to the involvement of the Ffestiniog Railway and a Heritage Lottery Fund grant of £4.3 million towards an estimated £9.1 million. The route from Rhyd Ddu to Porthmadog Harbour Station will be through Beddgelert, the Aberglaslyn Pass and across Pont Croesor. At the time of writing, the sections from Rhyd Ddu to Pont Croesor and Pen y Mount Crossover to Porthmadog Harbour are awaiting funding, but Pont Croesor to Pen-y-Mount Crossover is under construction. The latter involves the Welsh Highland Railway (Porthmadog) Ltd, which has an agreement with the Ffestiniog Railway for completing the route from Portmadog and, ultimately, operating trains on this stretch.

Snowdonia has a good network of railway lines compared with the rest of rural Britain, which is surprising given the mountainous terrain. The main lines hug the coast, and run up the Conwy and Aberdovey Valleys whilst the preserved lines generally take more spectacular routes in the mountains. The main line system was partly developed to transport the slate and other minerals by transhipment from the local narrow gauge railways. This inter-linking is now mutually beneficial to the viability of the rail system.

It is recommended that walkers take the train to the start point of a walk. Walkers should also make the decision before buying tickets whether, on the preserved railways, to travel the full length of the line and leave the train on the return trip. The preserved lines tend to finish running relatively early in the day and, except in summer, tend to be infrequent. Use of the trains may enforce a later start than would otherwise be chosen on shorter, winter days and this should be borne in mind when undertaking the longer walks.

It is obviously necessary to have current timetables which can be obtained at the relevant railway or at tourist information centres. Preserved railways review their timetables annually and the other lines usually issue new timetables twice each year. There may be special offers which will reduce fares, such as family tickets, or rover tickets sold by the "Great Little Trains of Wales" consortium.

Many of the stations are request stops – otherwise known as halts. At these it is necessary to indicate to the driver that you wish to board the train to ensure that it stops. Likewise it is also essential to tell the conductor or guard that you wish to leave the train at a halt to ensure that the train does stop.

The railways offer the opportunity to shorten walks or to see more remote areas in the region than could otherwise be comfortably accessed in a day. The linear walks in this book enable walkers to cross mountain ranges or undertake lengthy walks with less significant height gain. As many of the railway lines are at or near sea level the opportunity for downhill walks is less than might be expected. Brief details of places of interest passed during the walks are included. This may whet the appetite to tour castles etc. and more detailed information is usually available at the site concerned.

Acknowledgements

I am grateful for the assistance provided by these railway companies and, in particular, Peter Austin Secretary of The Great Little Trains of Wales. Last but not least, my thanks to my wife Jan for her help and support every step of the way.

Contents

The Railways

Bala Lake Railway 1
Brecon Mountain Railway 1
Cambrian Coast Line between Machynlleth and Pwllheli 2
Chester – Holyhead Coast Line 2
Conwy Valley Line 2
Fairbourne and Barmouth Steam Railway 2
Ffestiniog Railway 3
Llanberis Lake Railway 4
Talyllyn Railway 4
Vale of Rheidol Railway 5
Welshpool and Llanfair Light Railway 6
Welsh Highland Railway 6

The Walks

Walk 1: Pont-y-Pant to Dolwyddelan 8
Distance: 1.5 miles (2.4 kilometres)

Walk 2: Dolwyddelan to Roman Bridge via the Castle 10
Distance: 3 miles (4.8 kilometres)

Walk 3: Penllyn to Gilfach Ddu 13
Distance: 3.5 miles (5.6 kilometres)

Walk 4: Penrhyn to Tan-y-Bwlch 16
Distance: 3.5 miles (5.6 kilometres)

Walk 5: Bala to Llangower 19
Distance: 4 miles (6.4 kilometres)

Walk 6: Brynglas to Tywyn 22
Distance: 5 miles (8 kilometres)

Walk 7: Aberdovey to Tywyn 25
Distance: 5 miles (8 kilometres)

Walk 8: Pont-y-Pant to Betws-y-Coed via Llyn Elsi 28
Distance: 5 miles (8 kilometres)

Walk 9: Waunfawr to Dinas 32
Distance: 5.5 miles (8.8 kilometres)

Walk 10: Pen-y-Mount to Porthmadog 36
Distance: 5.5 miles (8.8 kilometres)

Walk 11: Penmaenmawr to Llanfairfechan 40
Distance: 5.5 miles (8.8 kilometres)

Walk 12: Talsarnau to Harlech   **43**
Distance: 6 miles (9.7 kilometres)

Walk 13: Nant Gwernol to Dolgoch Falls   **47**
Distance: 6 miles (9.7 kilometres)

Walk 14: Talycafn to Conwy   **51**
Distance: 6.5 miles (10.5 kilometres)

Walk 15: Waunfawr to Caernarfon   **55**
Distance: 7 miles (11.3 kilometres)

Walk 16: Blaenau Ffestiniog to Tan-y-Bwlch via Dduallt   **58**
Distance: 7 miles (11.3 kilometres) or 2.5 miles (4 kilometres)

Walk 17: Rhydyronen to Aberdovey   **62**
Distance: 7.5 miles (12.1 kilometres)

Walk 18: Llanrwst to Betws-y-Coed   **66**
Distance: 8 miles (12.9 kilometres)

Walk 19: Snowdon Ranger Youth Hostel to Waunfawr   **71**
Distance: 8 miles (12.9 kilometres)

Walk 20: Nant Gwernol to Morfa Mawddach   **75**
Distance: 8 miles (12.9 kilometres)

Walk 21: Dolwyddelan to Betws-y-Coed   **79**
Distance: 8.5 miles (13.7 kilometres)

Walk 22: Conwy to Penmaenmawr   **83**
Distance: 8.5 miles (13.7 kilometres)

Walk 23: Llanfairfechan to Bangor   **87**
Distance: 9 miles (14.5 kilometres)

Walk 24: Dyffryn Ardudwy to Barmouth   **91**
Distance: 9 miles (14.5 kilometres)

Walk 25: Fairbourne to Barmouth   **96**
Distance: 9.5 miles (15.3 kilometres)

Walk 26: Talycafn to Llanfairfechan   **101**
Distance: 11 miles (17.7 kilometres)

Walk 27: Dduallt to Tan-y-Bwlch via Tomen-y-mur   **105**
Distance: 11 miles (17.7 kilometres)

Walk 28: Pontsticill to Pant   **110**
Distance: 4 miles (6.4 kilometres)

Walk 29: Nantyronen to Aberystwyth via Capel Bangor   **114**
Distance: 7.5 miles (12.1 kilometres) or 5 miles (8 kilometres)

Walk 30: Llanfair Caereinion to Welshpool via Castle Caereinion 117
Distance: 10.5 miles (16.9 kilometres) or 4 miles (6.4 kilometres)

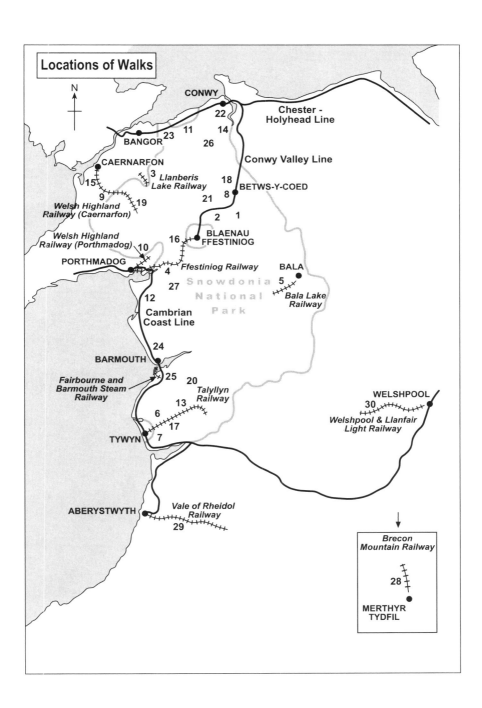

The Walks & The Railways

For ease of reference, the walks are grouped here under the railways used for the walks. Several walks involve two railways and are therefore listed under both of the railway lines. Walks numbered 1 to 27 in Snowdonia are ordered by the length of walk, number 1 being the shortest. The '**Bonus walks**' – 28, 29 and 30 – use preserved railways that are outside Snowdonia but are also members of The Great Little Trains of Wales consortium.

Bala Lake Railway
Walk 5: Bala to Llangower

Brecon Mountain Railway
Walk 28: Pontsticill to Pant

Cambrian Coast Line
Walk 7: Aberdovey to Tywyn
Walk 12: Talsarnau to Harlech
Walk 17: Rhydyronen to Aberdovey
Walk 20: Nant Gwernol to Morfa Mawddach
Walk 24: Dyffryn Ardudwy to Barmouth
Walk 25: Fairbourne to Barmouth

Chester – Holyhead Line
Walk 11: Penmaenmawr to Llanfairfechan
Walk 14: Talycafn to Conwy
Walk 22: Conwy to Penmaenmawr
Walk 23: Llanfairfechan to Bangor
Walk 26: Talycafn to Llanfairfechan

Conwy Valley Line
Walk 1: Pont-y-Pant to Dolwyddelan
Walk 2: Dolwyddelan to Roman Bridge via the Castle
Walk 8: Pont-y-Pant to Betws-y-Coed via Llyn Elsi
Walk 14: Talycafn to Conwy
Walk 18: Llanrwst to Betws-y-Coed
Walk 21: Dolwyddelan to Betws-y-Coed
Walk 26: Talycafn to Llanfairfechan

Fairbourne and Barmouth Steam Railway
Walk 25: Fairbourne to Barmouth

Ffestiniog Railway
Walk 4: Penrhyn to Tan-y-Bwlch
Walk 16: Blaenau Ffestiniog to Tan-y-Bwlch via Dduallt
Walk 27: Dduallt to Tan-y-Bwlch via Tomen-y-mur

Llanberis Lake Railway
Walk 3: Penllyn to Gilfach Ddu

Talyllyn Railway
Walk 6: Brynglas to Tywyn
Walk 13: Nant Gwernol to Dolgoch Falls
Walk 17: Rhydyronen to Aberdovey
Walk 20: Nant Gwernol to Morfa Mawddach

Vale of Rheidol Railway
Walk 29: Nantyronen to Aberystwyth via Capel Bangor

Welshpool and Llanfair Light Railway
Walk 30: Llanfair Caereinion to Welshpool via Castle Caereinion

Welsh Highland Railway (Caernarfon)
Walk 9: Waunfawr to Dinas
Walk 15: Waunfawr to Caernarfon
Walk 19: Snowdon Ranger Youth Hostel to Waunfawr

Welsh Highland Railway (Porthmadog)
Walk 10: Pen-y-Mount to Porthmadog

The Railways

This section provides a brief history of each of the railway lines used in these walks, together with the historic rolling stock that may be seen on the preserved railways. The railways are listed alphabetically; more detailed information can be obtained from bookshops at the preserved railways, tourist information centres and main stations.

Bala Lake Railway

This 600mm (1ft 11¾in) narrow gauge line runs on the old track bed of the standard gauge line between Ruabon and Barmouth Junction, now Morfa Mawddach on the Cambrian Coast Line. Opened in 1868, it was originally part of the Great Western Railway network and closed in 1965, one of many lines which closed in the reorganisation planned by Dr Beeching. Volunteers developed the 4½-mile lakeside, and fairly level, line between Llanuwchllyn and Bala in the period 1971/6.

The coal-fired steam engines are Holy War (1902), Maid Marian (1903) from Dinorwig Quarry, and Triassic (1911) from Rugby Cement. All passenger trains are normally steam-hauled.

Brecon Mountain Railway

Enthusiasts started this completely new 1ft 11¾in-gauge line in the 1970s utilising the trackbed of the Brecon and Merthyr Tydfil, which closed in 1964. Initially 1¾ miles in length between Pant and Ponsticill stations, it has recently been extended to Dolygaer (3½ miles) although there are still only the two points at which the train can be boarded. The railway carries tourist traffic through the Brecon Beacons National Park, where there is no competition from other steam railways.

The workhorse has been Graf Schwerin-Lowitz (1908) from East Germany, latterly supported by No. 2 (1930), an American locomotive used on a mineral railway in South Africa until 1974. No. 77, a very powerful German Garrett also from South Africa, is being renovated to replace Graf Schwerin-Lowitz on the steep gradients of the fully extended line to the top of the Torpantau Tunnel.

Cambrian Coast Line between Machynlleth and Pwllheli

The first section of line between Aberdovey and Barmouth was constructed by the Aberystwith and Welch Coast Railway in 1865. Cambrian Railways, on acquiring the company, extended the line to Pwllheli and Machynlleth in 1867. They were forced to cross the Dyfi Estuary nearer Machynlleth than had been originally intended and connected the line to Aberystwyth. Cambrian was absorbed by GWR and in turn by BR. The operating company is now Wales and Borders Trains using diesel standard 4ft 8⅜ in-gauge stock.

Chester – Holyhead Coast Line

The Chester and Holyhead Railway Company opened the line between Chester and Bangor in 1848, extended to Holyhead in 1850 with the opening of the Britannia Bridge over the Menai Strait. The line was absorbed into LNWR in 1859 then LMS and BR. Local services are now operated by First North Western using modern diesel standard gauge stock.

Conwy Valley Line

The Conwy and Llanrwst Railway opened in 1863, almost immediately taken over by the LNWR and gradually extended to Blaenau Ffestiniog by 1879. Subsequently LNWR was absorbed by LMS which, in turn, became part of BR. With the break-up of BR this line is now part of the First Northwestern Network. The diesel stock is unremarkable and standard gauge.

Fairbourne and Barmouth Steam Railway

This line was built in 1890 between Penrhyn Point and Fairbourne to transport building materials for the development of Fairbourne. Originally horse-drawn with a gauge of 2ft, in 1915 it was converted by its owners (then associated with Bassett-Lowke, the model railway manufacturers) to 15-inch gauge and steam-hauled. As might be expected, the locomotive, Prince Edward of Wales, was a Bassett-Lowke. The line was closed briefly in the 1980s when the gauge was converted to a miniature 12¼-inch gauge and the line is now 2½ miles in length.

Four new coal-fired steam engines were introduced in 1986, when the gauge was significantly reduced; these are half-scale replicas of Lynton & Barnstaple, Leek & Manifold and North Wales Narrow Gauge tank engines and a Darjeeling and Himalayas tender engine. The railway has diesel engines but trains are normally steam-hauled.

Ffestiniog Railway

The line between Porthmadog and Blaenau Ffestiniog is 13½ miles long, climbing 700 feet around some very tight bends, through tunnels and completing a complete spiral at one point. The line was opened in 1836 as a gravity railway to run wagons full of slate from the quarries around Blaenau Ffestiniog to Porthmadog for tranship-ment to sailing ships in the harbour there. Previously, the slate was taken by packhorse to Maentwrog and also transhipped onto barges for transport down river to Porthmadog.

Trains were steam-hauled from 1863 though the original 1ft 11½in gauge was retained. The more powerful and unique double Fairlie engines able to negotiate the tight bends were introduced from 1870, being built locally at Boston Lodge. The line was commercially very successful for the next 50 years, carrying both freight and passenger traffic. The railway closed in 1946 as the use of slate declined and road transport became more popular. The preserved line reopened gradually starting from Porthmadog in 1955 and reaching Dduallt in 1968.

The Tanygrisiau Reservoir blocked further reinstatement of the old track bed. This inspired the spiral, unique in Britain, which enabled the line to continue above the reservoir and rejoin the old track bed at Tanygrisiau Station in 1978. The line was extended into Blaenau Ffestiniog in 1982 where station facilities are shared with the Conwy Valley Railway.

Most trains are steam-hauled and exceptions are noted in the timetable. All of the steam engines are oil-fired to minimise the fire risk when passing through forestry. Those likely to be seen include: Merddin Emrys, a double Fairlie locomotive built in 1879; Linda and Blanche, both dating from 1893 (originally Penrhyn Quarry engines); and Mountaineer, built in 1917. Princess and Welsh Pony dating from 1867 can be seen at Porthmadog Station but are no longer in service.

Llanberis Lake Railway

The Padarn Railway was built in 1849 to transport slate from the great Dinorwig Quarry, the largest in the World, to the Menai Strait for transhipment at the purpose-built harbour of Port Dinorwig. This replaced the laborious transporting of slate 9 miles to the coast by a combination of boat along Llyn Padarn, packhorse and latterly a horse tramway.

The gauge of the original railway was an unusually broad 4ft. The quarry railway closed in 1961 and the quarry in 1969. A 600mm (1ft 11½in) fairly common narrow gauge line, largely on the old track bed was built in 1970-2. A short extension, taking the end of line closer to Llanberis and the Snowdon Railway, was completed in 2003.

The coal-fired steam engines are all part of the original stock from the quarry or harbour areas and were converted from a unique gauge of 1ft 10¾in: Elidir (1889); Thomas Bach (1904); and Dolbadarn (1922). Fire Queen, one of the original engines, is in the railway museum at Penrhyn Castle. All trains are normally steam-hauled.

Talyllyn Railway

The line from Tywyn to Nant Gwernol is just over 7¼ miles in length, rising some 300 feet and passing over the superbly propor-tioned viaduct which spans the Dolgoch gorge. The gauge is 2ft 3in, being the same unusual gauge as the Corris Railway which ran between 1879 and 1948 in the next valley. A short length of the Corris Railway has been reopened in the last couple of years.

The railway dates from 1865 and was built to transport slate from the bottom of the tramway that extended from the Bryneglwys Quarry into the Nant Gwernol valley. It now seems to have been an over-ambitious project just to exploit one quarry but the owners believed that there were large reserves of high quality slate and even gold. Hopes were soon dashed and output declined rapidly, the quarry eventually closing in the 1940s. At that time, the top end of the line was at Abergynolwyn Station with a mineral line extension running to Nant Gwernol.

The line was extended for passenger traffic into the Nant Gwernol Gorge in 1976 by the volunteer railway preservation society that took over the line in 1950. At Tywyn slate was transhipped onto the Aberystwith and Welch Coast (now the Cambrian) Railway and to a main line network established in the decade prior to 1865.

This route replaced a packhorse route through and over the mountain to Pennal, then down the Dyfi for transhipment to sea-going craft at Aberdyfi, and later using a route through Tywyn.

Continuous use of the railway results in many original engines still being in use today, including Talyllyn (1864), Dolgoch (1866), Sir Haydn (1878), Edward Thomas (1921) – the latter two being originally Corris Railway stock – and the slim Douglas (1918) built for a gauge of 2ft. These engines, along with Tom Rolt, which dates from 1948, are still coal-fired and haul all passenger trains. All of the original carriage stock dating from 1866 is still in use. When coupled to an original loco, this forms what is believed to be the world's longest-running original passenger train.

Vale of Rheidol Railway

This railway opened in 1902 primarily to serve the lead ore, timber and passenger traffic of the Rheidol valley. By 1930 the freight traffic had ceased and the winter passenger service was abandoned leaving the railway to survive on the summer tourists traffic between April and October.

The line had always struggled for survival under its previous owners. Although built and operated by a private company, the line was acquired by the Cambrian Railways in 1913, GWR in 1923 and, post war by BR. It was the last British Rail line to operate steam locomotives and was the first to be privatised in 1989. It is now owned and operated by a charitable company.

Throughout the history of the line, the gauge has been 1ft 11½in and the 11¾ miles of track climbs some 640 feet to Devil's Bridge, ultimately on a 1 in 50 gradient. When under GWR ownership, the railway was re-equipped with three new steam locomotives, Owain Glyndwr and Llywelyn in 1923, and Prince of Wales in 1924; the sixteen carriages all date from 1923 and 1938. Having been converted to oil-fired, these locomotives and carriages are all still in use today.

Welshpool and Llanfair Light Railway

Originally 9 miles long, connecting Llanfair Caereinion to the main line on the east side of Welshpool, the 8 miles of track now terminate at Raven Square on the west side of town, the track through town being lost to development in the 1950s. The 2ft 6in-gauge line was opened in 1903 solely to carry local freight such as coal, stone and livestock. The track has some short steep gradients – up to 1 in 29. Passengers were carried only until 1931.

Construction followed the Light Railways Act of 1895, which simplified both the construction and operation of lines such as this and the Vale of Rheidol Railway (which originally operated under the same ownership). Enthusiasts anticipated closure in 1956 but it took them until 1963 to reopen the line over the 4 miles between Llanfair and Castle Caereinion, and until 1981 to reach Welshpool (Raven Square).

The two original Beyer Peacock engines, Earl and Countess, are still on the line supported by Monarch (1953), Dougal (1946), the French-built Sir Drefeldwyn (1944), Californian-built Joan (1927), ex-Sierra Leone Railway no. 85 now numbered 14 (1954) and, more recently, no. 5/15 Orion (1948). The oldest coaches by far are four-wheeled carriages, the earliest dating from 1901 and obtained from the Zillertalbahn in Austria.

Welsh Highland Railway

The North Wales Narrow Gauge Railway opened the line from Dinas to Rhyd Ddu in 1872 using a gauge of 1ft 11½in. The line was extended to Porthmadog in 1923. This coincided with the decline of the slate quarries and increased use of the roads, causing the line to close in 1937. The length of the line was 22 miles, stopping 3 miles short of Caernarfon.

A three-quarter-mile length of track at the Porthmadog end of the line was reopened by an independent group of volunteers in 1980, and from 2003 began to be progressively extended to Pont Croesor. Coal-fired steam engines currently deployed on this section include:

an original Welsh Highland Railway loco, Russell (1906); Karen (1942) and Gelert (1953), both originally employed in Africa; Moel Tryfan (1953); and Pedemoura (1924).

In 1997, under the management of the Ffestiniog Railway, the rebuilding of the line from Caernarfon commenced with the construction of the 3 miles between Caernarfon and Dinas. The line was subsequently extended to Waunfawr, and on to Rhyd Ddu in 2003. The final stages of this exciting project are the rebuilding of the link through Beddgelert and the Aberglaslyn Pass, and to re-establish the link between the two stations in Porthmadog, which existed briefly in the 1930s.

Oil-fired Garratt steam engines from South African Railways and Prince (1863), from the Ffestiniog Railway, are utilised on this section. Connecting the lines would obviously facilitate the deployment of other Ffestiniog stock.

Walk 1: Pont-y-Pant to Dolwyddelan

Conwy Valley Line

Starting point: Station car park at Dolwyddelan off the A496 in the centre of the village.

Distance: 1.5 miles (2.4 kilometres)

Height gain: 30 feet (10 metres)

Relevant maps: Explorer OL18 (Harlech, Porthmadog & Bala) Landranger 115 (Snowdon)

Facilities: Café, inn and toilets in Dolwyddelan.

Terrain: Quiet lane or firm track all the way, virtually level ground. Very obvious route.

Take the train from Dolwyddelan to Pont-y-Pant, both request stops. Indicate to the driver the wish to board the train and advise the conductor promptly that you need to alight at Pont-y-Pant. This very short walk can also be used to extend the walk from Dolwyddelan to Roman Bridge by taking the train from Roman Bridge to Pont-y-Pant.

The old tramway track bed crosses the valley....

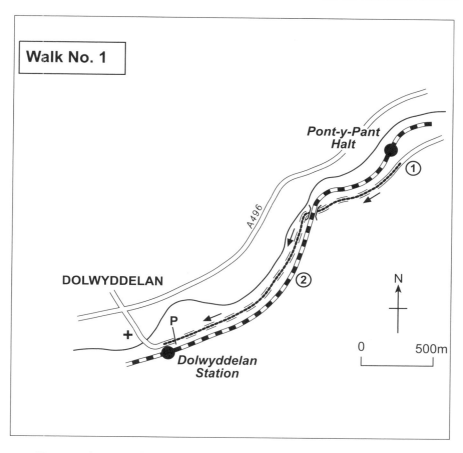

1. Turn right out of the halt at Pont-y-Pant to the end of the narrow lane. Follow the obvious stony track, and after about a half-mile pass under the railway line.

   After a further quarter-mile you reach a junction of paths indicated by a finger post. The causeway to the right was built on piers of slate bridged with massive slate slabs; it was part of a tramway that ran from a slate quarry in the hills above, down to the mill on the opposite side of the river.

2. Carry on along the track which, after another quarter-mile, passes through a farmyard to Dolwyddelan Station.

Walk 2: Dolwyddelan to Roman Bridge via the Castle

Conwy Valley Line

Starting point: Small station car park at Roman Bridge off the A496 about 1 mile west of Dolwyddelan.

Distance: 3 miles (4.8 kilometres)

Height gain: 400 feet (120 metres)

Relevant maps: Explorer OL18 (Harlech, Porthmadog and Bala), Landranger 115 (Snowdon)

Facilities: Inn, café and toilets in Dolwyddelan.

Terrain: Mainly firm tracks and easy route finding. Modest climb out of Dolwyddelan.

Take the train from Roman Bridge to Dolwyddelan, both of which are halts. Therefore, indicate clearly that you wish to board the train and advise your destination promptly to the conductor.

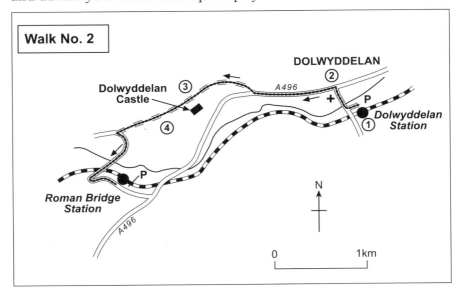

Sarn Helen, the Roman road, crossed the River Lledr at Pont-y-Pant but Roman Bridge, paradoxically, has no known connection with the Romans.

1. Turn left out of the station car park and right across the river, past St Gwyddelan's Church.

   St Gwyddelan's Church dates from the 16th century and also houses a 7th-century Celtic bell. The church is almost hidden by mature trees and is usually locked preventing access.

2. Turn left up the main road out of the village and past a lay-by. 150 metres further on bear right up a gated track. Fork right at a junction and climb to Dolwyddelan Castle mound.

   Construction of this castle was started in 1173 by Iowerth, father of Llewelyn the Great, who was born in the same year. The latter strengthened the fortifications during his reign. It was captured by Edward I in 1283 and maintained until the 16th century, after which it deteriorated into a ruin. Maredudd ap Ievan, who occupied the castle in the late 15th century, built the village church where his effigy can be seen and he also owned Gwydir Castle near Llanrwst. The keep was restored in the 19th century and it is still possible to climb to the top from where there is a superb panoramic view.

The keep of Dolwyddelan Castle

3.   Walk straight on along a faint track past the base of the mound (rather than the obvious track to the right). The track becomes clearer, climbing the hill ahead.

4.   Cross the ladder stile at the top of the hill where the track levels off then descends through a farmyard. Turn left along the lane winding across the valley across the river and railway line. Follow the lane bending sharply left back to the station.

Walk 3: Penllyn to Gilfach Ddu

Llanberis Lake Railway

Starting point: Gilfach Ddu which is the station by the Slate Museum where there is a large car park (fee).

Distance: 3.5 miles (5.6 kilometres)

Height gain: negligible!

Relevant maps: Explorer OL17 (Snowdon & Conwy Valley) Landranger 115 (Snowdon)

Facilities: Café and toilets at Gilfach Ddu and a range of facilities in nearby Llanberis

Terrain: Tracks, country lane and a few fields at the end of the walk. Firm, virtually level, ground and an obvious route.

Local information: The railway is just one of many attractions around a village which used to provide the labour for one of the largest slate quarries in the world, extending over 1500ft up the side of Elidir Fach. Other tourist features include the Snowdon Mountain Railway, Llyn Padarn Country Park and quarry hospital, a boat trip on Llyn Padarn, the Welsh Slate Museum, Dinorwig pumped storage power station (Electric Mountain), the remains of the 13th-century Dolbadarn Welsh Castle and, 2 miles away, the Victorian Bryn Bras Castle.

Advise the guard that you wish to leave the train at Penllyn. Following a recent extension of the line to Llanberis, the train first goes to Llanberis and halts to run the engine round the carriages in order to pull the train to the far end of the lake, Penllyn, where the train makes its next stop. Get off at this point, though there is no station or platform and passengers are discouraged from leaving the carriages. Alight on the opposite side to the lake so as not to cross the track in the path of the engine, which runs around the train for the return to Gilfach Ddu.

1. Walk alongside the track to cross the ladder stile at the end of the line and continue along the disused track bed to the lane. Bear left along the lane and turn left at the T-junction over Pen-y-llyn Bridge.

Walk No. 3

2. Turn left up the disused section of road over three ladder-stiles and bear left along the pavement alongside the A4086. Turn left through the gap in the stone wall and go down the stepped path to the track bed of an old railway line.

This was the main line between Llanberis and Caernarfon. It is now the Lon Las Peris cycle track as well as being a walkway.

3. Turn left, away from the railway tunnel, and later pass a small lake to the right formed when the railway embankment was constructed across an inlet of Llyn Padarn. Pass under a wrought iron footbridge to reach Y Glyn recreation area.

Steaming through Gilfach Ddu

4. Bear left by the toilet block to join a footpath running alongside the service road which converges with the road nearing the A4086 again. Bear left along the road to the far end of the Village car park and bear left again along the lakeside path. Cross a footbridge, a footbridge/stile combination, and then go through a kissing gate. At the head of the lake turn left over another footbridge and turn left again back to the station and car park.

Walk 4: Penrhyn to Tan-y-Bwlch

Ffestiniog Railway

Starting point: Tan-y-Bwlch Station car park, signposted off the A496 by the Oakeley Arms.

Distance: 3.5 miles (5.6 kilometres)

Height gain: 500 feet (150 metres)

Relevant maps: Explorer OL18 (Harlech, Porthmadog and Bala), Landranger 124 (Dolgellau)

Facilities: Car park, café and toilets at Tan-y-Bwlch station.

Terrain: Obvious tracks/paths and country lane, some soft ground in the middle section. Gradual climb and a fairly clear route.

Take the train from Tan-y-Bwlch to Penrhyn. This is one of several alternative routes between the two stations. It has the advantage of glorious views towards Snowdon after climbing above the dense forestry.

'Blanche' hauling the train out of Porthmadog into Minffordd

1. Go down the ramp at the top end of the station buildings up the road and over the level crossing. After 50 metres turn right along the narrow lane, for about a half-mile, at the end of which is a farmstead, Rhiw Goch.

2. Go straight on through gates to the left of buildings and follow the stony track into woodland. Carry on along the clear path and soon fork left at a junction of paths. Walk on past ruins, where there is another junction of paths. Go forward again at the next junction of paths 75 metres further on.

    At this latter junction there are two posts, the smaller bearing the number 36. The path to the right is part of a network of courtesy or permissive paths in woodland down to the valley below. Maps of these paths, with numbered posts at most junctions, are available from information centres and Ffestiniog Railway stations.

3. Leave the woods by way of a kissing gate and follow the boundary fence to the right. There are glorious views of the mountains

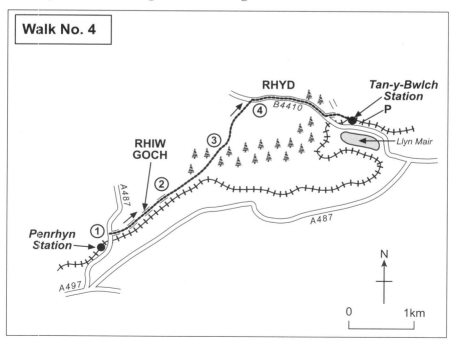

to the left in the next section of the walk which makes the climb out of the woodland worthwhile. Bear left across the stream in the valley, by a marker post, and along a faint path/track. Bear left away from the descending track and contour across the hill-side before climbing briefly to a gate. Go through the gate following the clear path alongside the stone wall to the right, to a lane and turn right through the hamlet of Rhyd.

4. Go along this lane for about half a mile past a car park then turn left up a narrow lane. At a sharp left-hand bend, turn right down the path to the station.

Walk 5: Bala to Llangower

Bala Lake Railway

Starting point: The car park and picnic site between the road and railway on the south side of the village of Llangower off the B4403.

Distance: 4 miles (6.4 kilometres)

Height gain: 550 feet (190 metres)

Relevant maps: Explorer OL23 (Cadair Idris & Bala Lake), Landranger 125 (Bala & Lake Vyrnwy, Berwyn)

Facilities: Toilets in car park by Llangower Halt, and a range of facilities in Bala.

Terrain: Paths and tracks, generally firm ground. Energetic climb for the first mile, and gradual descent. Easy route finding, with good views over Bala and the surrounding countryside.

Cross the railway line to the halt and take the train to the end of the line, which is a half-mile short of Bala town centre. Bala is one of the gateways to Snowdonia. The natural lake, being four miles long and the largest in Wales, is a focal point for water sports.

'Maid Marian' departing from Bala

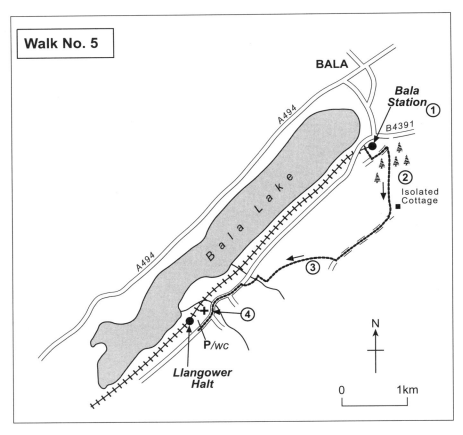

Walk No. 5

BALA

Bala Station ①

B4391

② Isolated Cottage

Bala Lake

A494

A494

③

+ ④

P/wc

Llangower Halt

N

0   1km

1. Cross the footbridge over the railway line, cross the ladder stile
    and bear right across a field. Cross another ladder stile in the
    right-hand top corner of the field and walk straight up the next
    field. Turn left along a track and bear left at a junction of tracks.
    After a further 150 metres, at the edge of the woodland turn
    sharply right up the clear path indicated by a finger post. Bear
    left up a forest track, and after 10 metres, bear left up a narrow
    but clear path. After about a quarter of a mile cross the stile over
    the boundary fence, leaving the woodland, and walk straight on.
    Bear right alongside a wire fence, as waymarked, to the next
    corner of the fence. Follow this fence uphill and cross the stile in
    the fence ahead.

For the next mile there are superb panoramic views of Bala and the lake, often filled with a colourful array of sailing dinghies.

2. Bear right across the next field to climb the stile in the right-hand top corner. Carry on alongside the fence to the right and cross the stile ahead. Go straight on, initially uphill, then cross fairly level, open moorland. Cross the ladder stile to the right of an isolated whitewashed stone cottage. Walk on to a marker post at the edge of a track and turn right along the track. Bear right at a junction of tracks and, after about 350 metres, bear left along a waymarked grassy path. At the end of this path bear left up a track and cross a ladder stile. Contour across the bottom corner of a field and cross a stile in the fence to the right. Carry on in the same direction, still contouring, to the ladder stile ahead.

3. Cross this ladder stile and descend gradually down the obvious path. Converge with and then continue alongside a fence. Cross the ladder stile by sheepfolds near a stream and turn right to follow the stream. Climb the ladder stile in the fence ahead and carry on alongside the stream. Turn left over a ladder stile to cross the footbridge over the stream. Walk straight on past a finger post, soon alongside a fence to the left and down to a road. Bear left along the road into Llangower.

Pass the stone church, not of great architectural interest, but still a good example of a simple and very attractive village church.

4. Carry on down the lane to the car park.

Walk 6: Brynglas to Tywyn

Talyllyn Railway

Starting point: Wharf station car park on the south side of Tywyn.

Distance: 5 miles (8 kilometres)

Height gain: none!

Relevant maps: Explorer OL23 (Cadair Idris & Bala Lake) Landranger 135 (Aberystwyth & Machynlleth)

Facilities: Inn *en route* in Bryncrug and a range of facilities in Tywyn. There is a market in Tywyn on Mondays.

Terrain: Tracks and quiet country lanes. Obvious route on firm level ground.

Take the train to Brynglas Halt, a short distance the other side of the Brynglas Ground Frame where the train will also stop. Advise the guard of your intention to leave the train. Access by the trains to sections of the single-track line involves the train on a particular section holding a token stored in the ground frame which is, therefore, a passing place for trains. Passengers should not attempt to board or leave the train at this point.

1. Turn right down the lane between the halt and the ground frame. Follow this lane for about a mile to the main road. Cross the road and go up the track opposite. Follow the track through a kissing gate and over a stream where the track deteriorates. Go straight on past a house and then bear right to cross a bridge/stile combination. Turn left alongside the stream; pass through the gap in the hedge ahead and walk straight on as the stream meanders to the left. Before reaching the field gate ahead, bear left soon walking alongside the stream again. Cross the ladder stile on the right and turn left into the centre of Bryncrug.

2. Bear left across the main road to go through the kissing gate in the stone wall and continue along the opposite bank of the stream. Cross several stiles and carry on along the embankment.

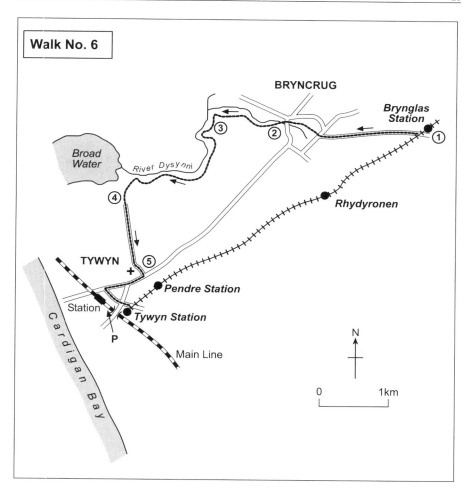

Turn left, still on the embankment, where the stream joins the River Dysynni.

3. Follow the embankment for a good mile alongside the Dysynni winding its way towards Broad Water. Ignore the path running away from the embankment just after passing woodland but, about a half-mile further on, just after passing the large farm on the opposite bank, bear left off the embankment through the gap in the fence as indicated by a finger post. Walk on by a hedge to

'Dolgoch' near Rhydyronen

the left and in the next field bear left to a finger post in the far corner of the field.

4.   Cross the bridge over the ditch and walk straight on to the church in Tywyn.

  St Cadfan's Church dates from the 6th century, and has a nave with massive Early Norman circular pillars. The tower fell in 1692 and the present tower dates from Victorian times. The 9th-century Cadfan stone, kept in the church, is said to bear the oldest known example of written Welsh and there are also effigies of an unnamed priest and a knight, dubbed the crying knight, dating from the 14th century.

5.   Turn right down the main street and turn left by the Cambrian Railway station to return to Wharf Station.

Walk 7: Aberdovey to Tywyn

Cambrian Coast Line

Starting point: Cambrian Railway Station car park in Tywyn. Not to be confused with the Talyllyn Railway Wharf Station, which is about 10 minutes walk up the road.

Distance: 5 miles (8 kilometres)

Height gain: 500 feet (150 metres)

Relevant maps: Explorer OL23 (Cadair Idris & Bala Lake), Landranger 135 (Aberystwyth & Machynlleth)

Facilities: Wide range of facilities in Aberdovey and Tywyn

Terrain: Tracks and foreshore. Virtually all of the climbing, initially steeply, is in the first mile to the reservoir. The latter half of the walk is very flat and the route finding should prove to be easy.

Local information: Historically, slate from Abergynolwyn quarry was transhipped at Wharf Station to the mainline railway. The main street of the old town stretches inland whilst the coastal area has been developed as a holiday resort with caravans and more permanent developments. The Church of St Cadfan on the Bryncrug road dates from Norman times but was heavily restored in 1844.

Take the train from Tywyn to Aberdovey (also spelt Aberdyfi) Station, which is just before the railway passes through the town. This pleasant little resort boasts two stations, the second (Penhelig) being on the other side of town. There is also a large car park in the centre as Aberdovey can be very crowded in peak season.

1. Walk out of the station and around the putting and bowling greens. Bear left across the main road and walk up Gwelfor Road. At the top of the hill cross the ladder stile on the left and bear right as indicated by the finger post. Follow the path along the side of the hill above houses climbing more gradually. Join the track on the right before reaching an isolated house and cross the ladder stile ahead. Carry on up the enclosed track, later metalled.

2. At the junction after passing the small reservoir, bear left still on the surfaced track. Bear left through the farmyard past the farmhouse, where the track deteriorates. Walk straight on along the top edge of a large field (ignoring the gate to the right opposite the first finger post). Pass through the next gate, in the far top corner of the field, and bear right initially alongside the fence as indicated by a finger post. Walk straight on as the fence bends right across the headland soon converging with the same fence. Turn left along a stony track, then bear right towards the sea.

3. Cross the main road by the cemetery and bear left down a track to cross the railway. Walk straight on across the fairway (being aware of golfers) to the foreshore and turn right towards Tywyn, which is about two miles away. Turn right almost immediately after reaching the promenade. Go straight on at the crossroads and over the railway bridge. Turn left by Wharf Station to the Cambrian Railway car park.

'Tom Rolt' waiting to leave Wharf Station

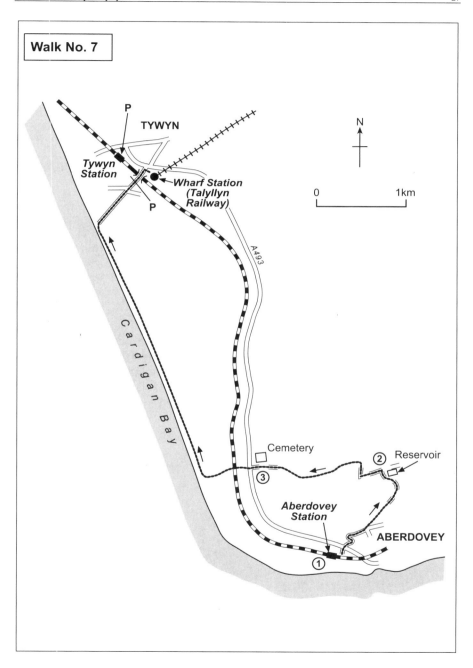

Walk No. 7

P

TYWYN

Tywyn Station

Wharf Station (Talyllyn Railway)

P

A493

N

0   1km

Cardigan Bay

Cemetery

② Reservoir

③

Aberdovey Station

ABERDOVEY

①

Walk 8: Pont-y-Pant to Betws-y-Coed via Llyn Elsi

Conwy Valley Line

Starting point: One of two car parks in front of Betws-y-Coed Station (if both are full, there is another at the top end of the village).

Distance: 5 miles (8 kilometres)

Height gain: 500 feet (150 metres)

Relevant maps: Explorer OL17 (Snowdon/Conwy Valley) & OL18 (Harlech, Porthmadog and Bala), Landranger 115 (Snowdon)

Facilities: The latter car park is passed at the end of the walk and there are public facilities near all of the car parks. There is a good range of facilities in Betws-y-Coed.

Terrain: Mainly tracks, generally firm ground. Progressive climb to Llyn Elsi, then increasingly steep descent. Fairly clear route.

Local information: Betws-y-Coed is the eastern gateway to Snowdonia, access being limited by the few crossings of the River Conwy. It is extremely popular in peak season both as a holiday centre and for refreshment en route to or from the National Park. The famous cast-iron Waterloo Bridge constructed by Thomas Telford in 1815 carries the A5 over the river. There are motor and railway museums and, surrounding the village, various features of interest. Walks in the area include some of these features.

Take the train from Betws-y-Coed to the halt at Pont-y-Pant. Be sure to ask the train conductor to stop the train at the halt.

1. Turn left out of the station along the narrow lane which soon crosses the railway line. Turn left at the junction of lanes and cross the Afon Lledr. Bear left across the main road (A470) through a handgate and bear left up the clear path. Cross a ladder stile and a stone stile at the end of the path to turn sharply right up a lane.

    This is part of Sarn Helen, a Roman road between Canovium in the

The miniature railway near Betws-y-Coed station

Conwy Valley and Tomen-y-mur near Trawsfynydd, parts of which, due south of Dolwyddelan, are also shown on maps. An alternative walk is to carry on along this track which becomes a lane emerging onto the A5 opposite the Miners' Bridge over the River Llugwy. There is a riverside path down the opposite bank of the river to Betws-y-Coed.

2. After half a mile, where the metalled lane bends right, walk straight on over a ladder stile and up the track ahead. Follow this track for little more than a mile, crossing another two ladder stiles and then a track. Latterly the track passes over level ground and then descends through two gates and between dilapidated buildings.

This is the abandoned quarry village of Rhiwddolion; quarries to the east and west are now hidden in the forestry plantations.

3. After climbing again briefly turn sharply right up a grassy track which is not waymarked – except by deduction from the "no cycles" sign. On reaching a stile in the forestry fence turn left (do

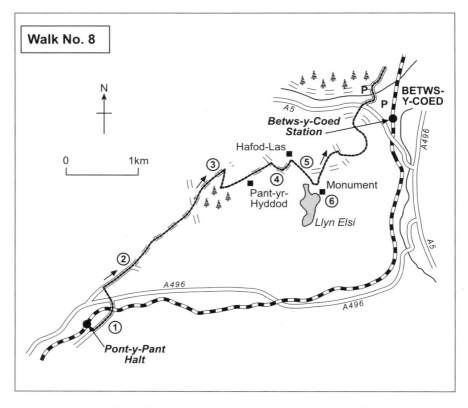

not cross the stile into the trees). Continue climbing over the mound ahead along a path, prompted by frequent marker posts. Descend to the left of a small farmstead (Pant-yr-hyddod) and pass through a kissing gate. Join the track ahead at the end of which pass through a gate and turn right along a forest track.

4. Fork left and then turn left at ensuing junctions before turning sharply left downhill towards Hafod-las. Climb the ladder stile ahead and turn right opposite the farm along another track as indicated by a marker post. After 40 metres fork right and then bear right alongside the fence to the right, signed Llyn Elsi.

5. Cross this fence by way of a ladder stile and follow the dry stone wall to the left along the edge of trees. Carry on across a forest

track and bear right along the foot of a mound. Turn left up an improved path to the memorial.

This is a superb panoramic viewpoint overlooking Llyn Elsi with a backdrop of Moel Siabod and other peaks. The monument commemorates the opening of the Betws-y-Coed Waterworks, in 1914, supplied by Llyn Elsi.

6. Turn left down the path away from the memorial and lake. This well-worn path, improved in places, is the Jubilee Path to Betws-y-Coed. Cross a forest track and bear right still following the obvious path. Descend increasingly steeply crossing another forest track. Carry on down the clear winding, and sometimes steep, path. Where Betws-y-Coed can be glimpsed through the trees, follow the path bending left and briefly uphill before continuing the descent towards the A5. Turn left briefly down an intersecting track and, after only 30 metres, turn right leaving the track. After a further short steep descent turn right along the road into Betws-y-Coed.

Walk 9: Waunfawr to Dinas

Welsh Highland Railway (Caernarfon)

Starting point: Off-road parking (not an officially designated car park) is available in Dinas Station off the A487, half a mile north of its junction with the A499. *The station is locked at 5.00pm*.

Distance: 5.5 miles (8.8 kilometres)

Height gain: 430 feet (130 metres)

Relevant maps: Explorer OL17 (Snowdon & Conwy Valley), Landranger 115 (Snowdon)

Facilities: Inn near Waunfawr Station and toilets at Dinas Station. Range of facilities in Caernarfon.

Terrain: Field paths, tracks and country lanes, ground mostly firm. Energetic climb for the first mile then very gradual descent to Dinas. Route finding requires care at times, partly because there are so many footpaths!

Take the train from Dinas to Waunfawr.

1. Turn right across the footbridge and car park to the road and turn left. Turn right up the lane, signposted to Rhosgadfan, and continue up the principal lane at a sharp bend to cross a cattle grid. Bear right, leaving the lane, down to a stone wall at the end of which go straight on along a faint fairly level path. Carry on towards a single storey white building which comes into view over the crest of the hill. Pass through the kissing gate in the wall ahead by a prominent white post and bear left along an enclosed track past the previously mentioned building which is a stable block. There may well be miniature horses in the fields either side of the track.

2. At the end of the track turn right down a narrow lane past a cemetery. Where this lane bends sharply left go straight on through a kissing gate along the bottom side of a field. Cross a ladder stile to join another enclosed track which bends sharply

Beyer-Garratt 143 alongside the Lon Eifion path

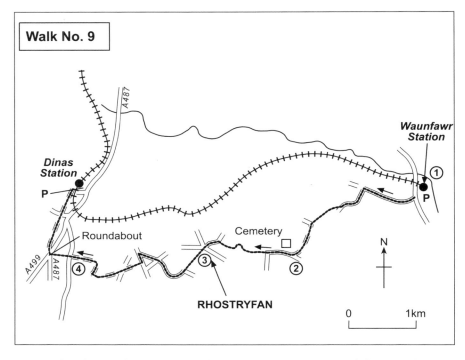

Walk No. 9

Waunfawr Station

Dinas Station

P

Roundabout

Cemetery

RHOSTRYFAN

N

0   1km

right then left through a farmyard. At the end of this track turn left down a lane into the village of Rhostryfan.

3. Go straight over the major road, down another lane and almost immediately bear left along the path down the side of the school. Go forward through a succession of kissing gates at the end of which carry on along a track. At the end of this track, bear right down a narrow winding lane. Turn left at the T-junction and after only 30 metres bear right. Turn left at the next T-junction and after 75 metres turn right down an enclosed track, going straight on where the track bends left. Go straight on at a junction of tracks and pass through the handgate on the right, opposite a house. Bear right across a field to the gate on the right side of woodland that is in the far bottom corner. Cross the adjacent stone stile to join an initially enclosed track which bends right then left over a brook. Carry on to the right of a farm along the side of the farmhouse to a road.

4.   Cross the road and go down the track opposite then go through the kissing gate by the field gate on the right. Carry on in the same direction and turn left through another kissing gate. Pass through the next kissing gate in the hedge ahead and bear right to cross the road on the right side of a roundabout. Bear right along the Lon Eifion cycle track back to Dinas Station.

Walk 10: Pen-y-Mount to Porthmadog

Welsh Highland Railway (Porthmadog)

Starting point: Welsh Highland Railway car park on the north side of Porthmadog

Distance: 5.5 miles (8.8 kilometres) – reduced by up to a mile after extension of the railway

Height gain: 650 feet (200 metres)

Relevant maps: Explorer OL18 (Harlech, Porthmadog and Bala), Landranger 124 (Dolgellau)

Facilities: Full range of facilities in Porthmadog

Terrain: Paths, tracks and country lanes. Energetic climb for about half a mile up a lane from Prenteg, and a steep descent into Tremadog. Some soft ground is likely to be encountered and, whilst route finding is generally easy, care is needed at the end of the track after passing the standing stone.

Take the Welsh Highland Railway train for the short trip to Pen-y-Mount station or, after extension of the line, to the far end of the line. Advise the guard where you wish to leave the train. The following instructions assume the walk starts from Pen-y-Mount.

1. Go through the kissing gate at the side of the station building and turn left along the enclosed path. Cross two tracks by way of kissing gates and continue alongside the railway track bed. Climb numerous stiles in the fences across the path, then cross a ladder stile and turn left down a track. Where this track bends left, cross the ladder stile on the right. Walk along the field margin with the fence to the left for about a half-mile, passing through a kissing gate, over a stile and between an old stone building and the wall. Go on between the wall and a ditch. Turn left through a handgate in the fence a few hundred metres short of the chapel ahead, and walk alongside the hedge to the left to the road.

'Karen' in the 'sheds' – access is included in the trip up the line

2. Go up the lane on the other side of the A498, climbing through the village of Prenteg. Follow this lane for over half a mile, then fork left at a junction and cross two cattle grids. Bear left down the waymarked stony track, winding and undulating for about a half-mile, and passing to the right of Fachgoch.

> *Soon after passing this property note the standing stone in the field to the left of the track. Such stones probably date from the Bronze Age or Stone Age. Judging by their position many could be route markers, but may also be memorials or boundary stones.*

3. Going through a gateway where the track bends sharply left downhill to another property, leave the track and walk straight on where initially there is no distinct path. After about 100 metres bear right alongside the wall ahead (do not go through the gap in the wall). At the corner of the wall bear slightly left to start the progressively steep descent, where the path again is not clear. After another 100 metres bear right down a clear path leading to an iron handgate in the stone wall beyond which the ground falls away steeply. Go through the gate and follow the

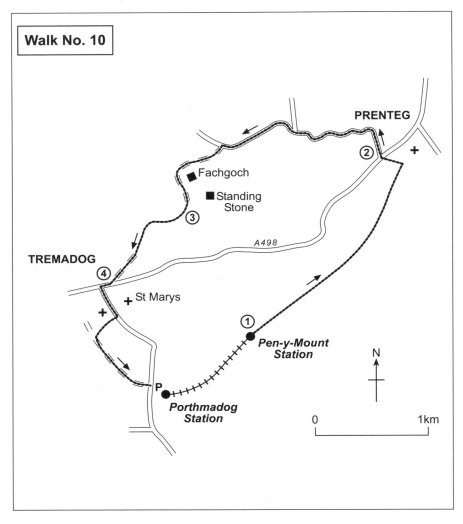

Walk No. 10

PRENTEG

② +

■Fachgoch

■Standing
Stone

③

A498

TREMADOG

④

+ St Marys

+

①

**Pen-y-Mount
Station**

N

P

Porthmadog
Station

0   1km

steep, stepped path, ford a stream, and then bear left alongside it
to cross the stile in a fence. Follow the clear path still descending by fences to the right then left and over a dilapidated stone
wall. Go through the handgate to a junction of lanes and walk
forward before turning right down the lane previously hidden
behind a hedge. At the bottom of this lane turn right along the
A498 to the centre of Tremadog.

This village, with its spacious square and solid buildings, was founded by William Madocks in 1805 and was also the birthplace of T.E. Lawrence (Lawrence of Arabia) in 1888.

4. Turn left through the square and past the de-consecrated church of St Mary. Turn right over the stone stile at the far corner of the boundary wall of a huge chapel. At the back corner of this wall, cross a footbridge and follow the path – now with a hedge to the left. Go through a kissing gate and turn left along a broad, straight surfaced track back to the station.

    This track was the route of a tramway from slate quarries in the hills above to Porthmadog Harbour.

Walk 11: Penmaenmawr to Llanfairfechan

Chester – Holyhead Line

Starting point: Station car park at Llanfairfechan

Distance: 5.5 miles (8.8 kilometres)

Height gain: 1380 feet (420 metres)

Relevant maps: Explorer OL17 (Snowdon/Conwy Valley), Landranger 115 (Snowdon)

Facilities: Inns, hotels and cafés in both towns. Toilets near to both stations.

Terrain: Fairly steep path to the stone circle; track and lane descending gradually into Llanfairfechan – straightforward route.

Local information: Llanfairfechan was historically a small coastal resort, now by-passed by the A55 along which traffic flows to the Lleyn Peninsula, Anglesey and Ireland.

Take the train from Llanfairfechan to Penmaenmawr.

> *The mountain towering over Penmaenmawr (which translates as 'large stone point') is scarred with old quarry workings. Vertiginous inclines for transporting the slate are still clearly visible. There is also evidence of ancient settlements including a prehistoric axe factory discovered in 1919 and the Druids Circle at the high point of this walk.*

1. Cross the footbridge over the railway and walk up the road opposite (Paradise Road). Go over the crossroads and, after 100 metres, bear right up the stepped path by flats. At the top of this path turn right to a road junction and turn left. After 30 metres bear left up an enclosed path. Turn right along Graiglwyd Road and then bear left up a farm track signposted to "Druids Circle". Bear left alongside the buildings and then bear right through a kissing gate. Follow the obvious path winding up the hill.

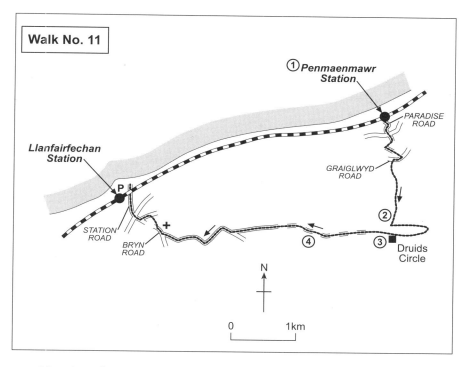

2. Nearing the top cross another path and then bear left along a paved section up to the kissing gate in the wall ahead. Go straight on through the kissing gate to the marker post and bear left along the clear track, joining the North Wales Path. Turn sharp right at the next marker post to climb up to the stone circle now in view.

> *The Druids Circle is a largely complete 50ft circle of stones, some up to 5 feet in height, in a commanding position with extensive views to the north and east. Druidism was the Celtic religion in pre-Roman times and such circles were typically constructed in the period 500-1800 BC. This one may be even older – legend would have us believe it was used in the worship of the goddesses Andras and Ceridwen.*

3. Follow the path to the right of the stone circle and the remains of another, less well-preserved, circle. Follow the path, contouring

The Druids Circle, high point of this walk

to converge very gradually with the North Wales Path. Carry on along the clear track, ignoring the path climbing to the right.

4. After about three-quarters of a mile, pass through the gate in the wall ahead, starting the descent with a glorious view of the Menai Straits below. Carry on along an enclosed farm track and then down a lane. Turn right at the T-junction, leaving the North Wales Path, to follow a lane winding down into Llanfairfechan.

    Turn right at the junction down Bryn Road, past a chapel, and, at the end of the pavement, bear right down an enclosed path. At the end of this path go down the street ahead at the end of which turn right down to the traffic lights. Cross the major road and go down Station Road. Pass under the A55 and railway line then immediately turn left to the station.

Walk 12: Talsarnau to Harlech

Cambrian Coast Line

Starting point: Harlech Station car park, off the A496 below the castle, near to the level crossing.

Distance: 6 miles (9.7 kilometres)

Height gain: 160 feet (50 metres)

Relevant maps: Explorer OL18 (Harlech, Porthmadog and Bala), Landranger 124 (Dolgellau)

Facilities: There is a range of facilities in Harlech.

Terrain: Principally tracks and some field paths, minimal climbing and firm ground. The route finding is generally easy.

Local information: Harlech Castle is the obvious focal point on a rocky outcrop rising 200 feet above the sea at the time it was completed by Edward I in 1289. It is still remarkably well-preserved considering its history – besieged in 1294/5, then taken by Owain Glyndwr in 1404, before being retaken in 1408 by the future Henry V. In 1468, after a seven-year siege, it was the last Lancastrian stronghold to fall in the Wars of the Roses . It was also the last Royalist castle to fall in the Civil War in 1647. By that time, it was becoming dilapidated and was then allowed to fall into ruin.

Take the train from Harlech to Talsarnau Halt. Advise the conductor that you wish to leave the train there.

1.　Go through the station car park and turn left over the railway line. Walk straight on along the enclosed track to the embankment and turn left along the embankment. Cross the bridge over a drainage ditch and carry on along the embankment. Do not cross the next fence ahead, where there is a junction of paths. Turn right, alongside this fence, cross a footbridge and turn right alongside an embankment.

2.　Turn right on reaching a lane by a cluster of houses and then turn left along an enclosed track. Pass through a kissing gate and turn left along the edge of a field. Bear left over the triangular stile in the corner of the field and walk up the next two fields with a hedge to the right. Bear left alongside the high wall of the churchyard and through a kissing gate.

Llanfihangel-y-Traethau (St Michael's on the Shores) is a delightful little church dating from the 12th century, and is beautifully situated on a mound which would have originally been an island. This is one of the less-famous St Michael's Mounts found in Britain and Brittany. There is an information board in the church porch. The monolithic pillar, bearing a Latin inscription also dating from the 12th century, is behind a yew tree about 10 metres away.

3.   Carry on walking around the churchyard wall and turn left by the wall ahead down steps. Climb the steps on the opposite side of the gully, pass through a kissing gate and continue climbing the bank. Bear right near the top of the bank past a marker stone. On reaching level ground, turn sharply left to pass to the right of a stone wall and then left again around the reservoir towards a farmstead. Bear right of the farm to pass through a field gate and turn right down a surfaced track.

There is a superb view from here across the estuary to Portmeirion and Porthmadog. Portmeirion was built in the Italianate or 'Mediterranean' style by a Welsh architect, Sir Clough

Looking north, Portmeirion in the middle distance

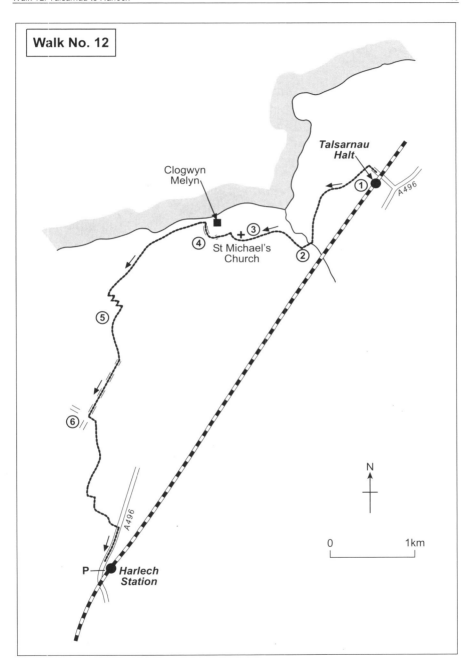

Williams-Ellis, starting in the 1920s and enlarged from 1954. Some of the older buildings have been rescued from other parts of the country (entry charge).

4.   Fork left at the junction of tracks. At the end of this track, by Clogwyn Melyn, turn left alongside the fence to the right and through the gap in the wall ahead. 100 metres further on, cross the ladder stile in the fence to the right and then continue in the same direction along a clear path through bracken between hillocks. Bear right to cross the ladder stile ahead. Bear right to contour around another hillock and, approaching a house, cross the ladder stile in the fence to the right. Carry on in the same direction across the front of the house, over the ladder stile ahead and then turn left along a track.

5.   Fork right at a junction of tracks through a farmyard and then bear left over a ladder stile. Cross the corner of a field and go through the gate ahead to carry on in the same direction, converging with a stone wall. Bear right alongside the wall, over a ladder stile and ahead alongside a conifer plantation. At the end of the plantation climb a ladder stile and cross a concrete track. Bear left to join a concrete track along the edge of woodland to the right.

6.   At a complex junction of concrete tracks turn left to a wire fence. Cross the adjacent stile and the field diagonally to the stile in the opposite fence. Continue in the same direction across the next field, over a ditch and stile, and on to the far corner of the third field. Cross another stile and bear right alongside the fence to the left. Cross a stile and go through the adjacent kissing gate. Bear left along the well-worn path over a drainage ditch and left through woodland. Pass through modern housing development in the direction of the castle and bear right along the A496 to the station car park.

Walk 13: Nant Gwernol to Dolgoch Falls

Talyllyn Railway

Starting point: Car park between the road and Dolgoch Station.

Distance: 6 miles (9.7 kilometres)

Height gain: 650 feet (200 metres)

Relevant maps: Explorer OL23 (Cadair Idris & Bala Lake), Landranger 124 (Dolgellau) and 135 (Aberystwyth & Machynlleth)

Facilities: Ample parking between the B4405 and Dolgoch Falls Station. Café at nearby Dolgoch Falls Hotel. Inn, café and toilets in Abergynolwyn en route.

Terrain: Mostly firm tracks and paths and a quiet country lane, though some soft ground over fields near the end of the walk. Undulating ground, the only climb of significance being at Birds' Rock. There is a short steep descent at the end of the walk. A fairly straightforward walk.

Before (or after) the main walk, be sure to take the short detour under a magnificent railway viaduct up to the falls. This is highly recommended.

Then, take the train from Dolgoch Falls to Nant Gwernol Station. This is the most attractive part of the line passing through Abergynolwyn Station, and up the side of the ravine to Nant Gwernol. This station, which does not have road access, is also a good starting point for walks up to the Bryn Eglwys slate quarry and the ridge, from which there are superb views to the south over the Dovey Estuary.

1. Walk past the end of the line along the level path and cross the gorge by way of the footbridge. Turn left and follow the obvious path down the gorge to a lane. Turn left down the lane into Abergynolwyn and turn left along the B4405.

    The village and railway were developed in the mid-nineteenth century with the opening of the quarry in the 1840s. At its peak the

'Edward Thomas' crossing the handsome viaduct at Dolgoch Falls

*quarry employed about 300 men, many of whom would have lived
with their families in Abergynolwyn.*

2. Turn right down the track between the playground and the
    stream. Cross the footbridge over the stream and follow the
    partly paved path bending right past cottages and up steps. Soon
    cross a ladder stile and follow the now obvious path above the
    stream crossing another two stiles. Fork left by a marker post
    above the landslip and then immediately fork right, descending
    to the stream. Carry on along the bank of the stream past the
    front of a cottage to the road.

    *The bridge over the stream is a good vantage point for a view of the
    tree-covered outcrop in the middle of the valley about three
    quarters of a mile up the lane. This is the site of Castell y Bere, a
    small native Welsh castle built by Llewellyn the Great in 1221. It
    was captured and garrisoned by the Edward I in 1283 but
    abandoned only a few years later. It is maintained as an ancient
    monument though entry is free. Whilst little of the structure remains,
    the mound is attractive. Further up the valley there is the lovely*

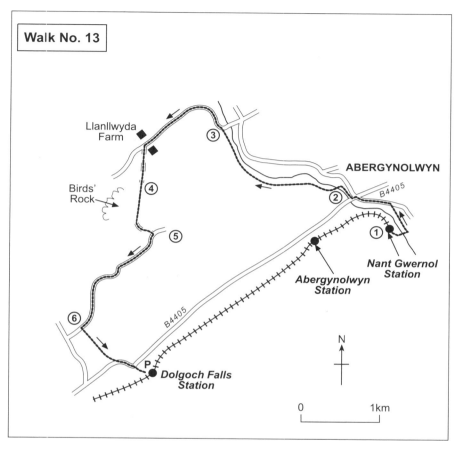

Walk No. 13

Llanllwyda Farm

③

ABERGYNOLWYN

B4405

Birds' Rock

④

②

①

Nant Gwernol Station

⑤

Abergynolwyn Station

⑥

B4405

N

P

Dolgoch Falls Station

0   1km

St Michael's Church which has a display in the vestry detailing the life of Mary Jones. At the end of the lane by the old bridge over the Cadair River, are the remains of her cottage and memorial. Born in 1784, at the age of 16 she walked barefoot the 25 miles to Bala in an attempt to buy a bible. Thomas Charles gave her three bibles and the incident inspired him to found the British and Foreign Bible Society.

3. Unless detouring up the valley, do not cross the bridge, but follow the lane ahead for a generous half-mile. About 100 metres after passing between the buildings of Llanllwyda Farm, turn left over a waymarked ladder stile. Bear left along the clear stony track climbing Birds' Rock – often called 'Bird Rock' (in Welsh, 'Craig Aderyn').

Although Birds' Rock is now some 4 miles from the coast and its base is only 20 feet above sea level, it is still a nesting ground for cormorants and other sea birds. This is because the sea has receded after many hundreds of years, but the birds still retain a memory of its original location. Charles Darwin stayed at nearby Plas Edwards and spent a great deal of time studying this unusual phenomenon. As a result of the Countryside Rights of Way (CROW) Act it may well be designated as open access land in 2005. Access will probably be conditional, however, as it is also a site of special scientific interest (SSSI).

4. This track deteriorates to a faint grassy track on passing through a field gate. The peak of Birds' Rock is to the right. Converge with the stone wall to the left, still climbing where the track is no longer evident. Bear left through another gate and follow the again faint track contouring across the field to join a clear track.

5. Turn right along a metalled track for about a mile passing between a cottage and outbuildings before descending steeply to follow the track through a farm.

6. 50 metres further on climb the stile by a finger post on the left and walk across two fields by the fence to the right. Contour across the next field to cross the fence ahead by way of a stile near an isolated oak tree. Go straight on to join the well-worn path, passing under another oak tree, with its attached waymarker, and then bear right downhill by the fence to the right. Near the bottom of the field, as the car park comes into view, bear left at a finger post by a gate in the fence. Contour across the field and complete the descent down another clear path below oak trees. Cross the stile by the bend in the road and turn left to the car park.

Walk 14: Talycafn to Conwy

Chester – Holyhead and Conwy Valley Lines

Starting point: Conwy station car park in the centre of town. If this is full there is a large car park off the B5106 after passing through the castle wall.

Distance: 6.5 miles (10.5 kilometres)

Height gain: 800 feet (240 metres)

Relevant maps: Explorer OL17 (Snowdon & Conwy Valley), Landranger 115 (Snowdon)

Facilities: Inn at Talycafn and wide range of facilities in Conwy

Terrain: Field paths, tracks and quiet lanes, undulating ground with no significant gradients. Route finding is fairly straightforward.

Local information: Conwy, as may be expected of a World Heritage Site, has a host of interesting features for the visitor. Highlights include the Castle, the curtain wall of the town, Plas Mawr, Aberconwy House, St Mary's Church, the quayside, Telford's suspension bridge and Stephenson's tubular railway bridge.

Take the train to Talycafn, changing at Llandudno Junction.

1. Cross the railway line and the bridge over the River Conwy. Turn right at the junction of lanes on the other side of the bridge. Climb gradually away from the river and then alongside woodland to the right. Turn left through a field gate by a waymarker and climb up the field to cross the stile by the gate near the top corner. Walk on by the fence to the left then straight on to the left of a mound. Cross the stile under the oak tree and turn left along the lane.

2. Where the lane bends sharply left go straight on up an enclosed path, then field to cross a ladder stile. Bear right past a ruined cottage and then descend alongside the fence to the right. Cross the ladder stile and turn left briefly along a busy road. Turn right by the telephone box down a partly surfaced track and turn

Local train passing alongside Conwy Castle

sharply right past a farm. Follow this track for about a half-mile to a T-junction and turn right along a lane to a church.

This isolated church is not noteworthy historically, but is attractive and memorable for its unusual octagonal bell tower.

3. Turn left down the field alongside the churchyard. Cross the footbridge over the Afon Gyffin and walk straight on by a hedge to the left. Turn right along a lane, turn right at a T-junction and then follow the lane bending right into the village of Henryd.

4. Turn left by the school and pass the cemetery. About half a mile out of the village, pass a junction of lanes and bear right up an enclosed waymarked path opposite Cyffredin Farm. At the end of this enclosed path go straight on through a handgate by a house. Pass through the kissing gate ahead and up a field to the road. Turn left along the road for 200 metres then turn sharply right up the caravan site access road.

5. At the bend, follow the waymarked path uphill. At the top of the

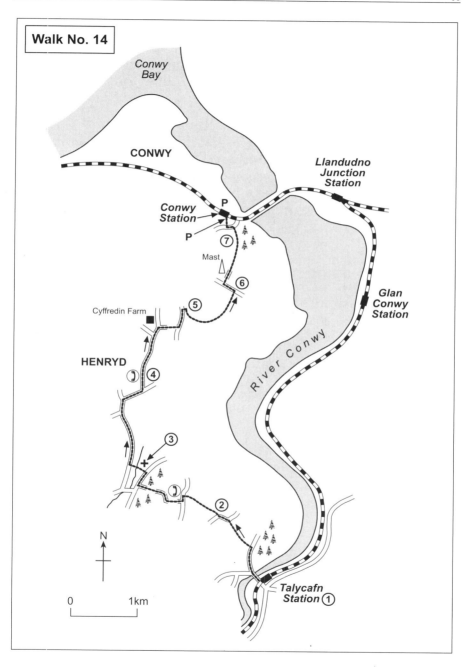

Walk No. 14

Conwy Bay

CONWY

Llandudno Junction Station

Conwy Station

P

P

⑦

Mast

⑥

⑤

Cyffredin Farm

Glan Conwy Station

River Conwy

HENRYD

④

③

②

N

0   1km

Talycafn Station ①

enclosed path cross a ladder stile and continue up the left-hand side of a field. On reaching the top corner cross another ladder stile and a surfaced track to join another enclosed path. Pass through a succession of kissing gates following the hedge on the right, which bends left then goes straight over the top of the hill to a lane.

6. Turn left down the lane for a short distance and then turn right up a track past the mast. Bear right around the farm track then go straight on through a kissing gate along the track, generally enclosed. Follow the track through the gap in the hedge to the left and continue in the same direction with the hedge now to the right. Climb the ladder stile at the end of this track and bear left to pass through a kissing gate and stile combination at the corner of woodland. Follow the well-worn path along the bottom edge of the woodland.

    Pause to enjoy the sight of the battlements of Conwy Castle without the clutter of later development – surely the best view of the castle. Like Caernarfon Castle, Conwy is irregularly shaped, being confined by the rocky outcrop which added to its fortifications. Both castles were built for Edward I by James of St George, starting in 1283. Edward I was besieged at Conwy during the Welsh uprising in 1294, and Richard II sought refuge there in 1399. The castle was held briefly by the Welsh in 1401 and saw action in the Civil War before being partly demolished in 1665, when the monarchy was restored.

7. Cross the stile in the fence to the left and drop down the field to turn left along a lane. Turn left along the road then go through the car park on the right and under the railway line. Bear left into Conwy and bear left again to the railway station car park.

Walk 15: Waunfawr to Caernarfon

Welsh Highland Railway (Caernarfon)

Starting point: Car park at Caernarfon Station (Welsh Highland Railway) signposted from main road. ***This car park is locked at 5pm*** – there is also a large public car park a short distance away, between the station and the castle.

Distance: 7 miles (11.3 kilometres)

Height gain: 300 feet (90 metres)

Relevant maps: Explorer OL17 (Snowdon & Conwy Valley), Landranger 115 (Snowdon)

Facilities: Inn near Waunfawr Station. Wide range of facilities in Caernarfon.

Terrain: Mostly firm tracks, short brisk climb then very gradual descent into Caernarfon. Easy route finding.

Local information: The castle is the obvious feature of interest. This massive medieval fortress dates from 1283, instigated like so many others by Edward I. Building was interrupted by rebels lead by Madog taking the fort in 1294, and it was not completed until 1330. It was garrisoned until the Tudor era and was partly dismantled about 1660, after the Civil War. The site of the Roman fort Segontium is also worth a visit.

Take the train from Caernarfon to Waunfawr.

1. Turn right across the footbridge and car park and turn left along the lane. Turn right up a lane signposted Rhosgadfan. Where the principal lane bends sharply left go straight on along a narrow lane which soon deteriorates to a track. Follow this fairly level track – generally enclosed, stony, then grass and later surfaced.

2. Turn right along the track alongside the railway line just before reaching the railway bridge, about 150 metres after passing over the bed of a disused branch line. Follow the track across the railway line to wind downhill and over the river. Turn left at a junc-

The massive Caernarfon Castle from the riverside, near to the
Welsh Highland Railway station

tion of tracks and follow the track bending right then left
through a farmyard. Fork left at a junction of tracks.

3.   About a quarter of a mile after passing through the farm, and
     before reaching a surfaced lane, turn left through a field gate.
     The relevant waymarker is not obvious being above eye level on
     the gatepost. Bear left across the field through the gap in the wall
     and turn right. Climb the metal ladder stile in the hedge ahead
     and bear left to cross the stile in a wire fence. Bear left again to
     cross the ladder stile at the end of the hedge and go alongside the
     wall to the left. Join the enclosed path ahead, through several
     sharp bends, for over half a mile. At the end of the track, bear
     right through the grounds of Pandy Bach and join a lane along-
     side a stream into Bontnewydd. Turn right along the A487
     briefly and then turn left down the lane signposted Lon Eifion.

     *Lon Eifion is a 12½-mile cycleway utilising old railway lines between
     Caernarfon and Bryncir (a village about 7 miles north-west of
     Porthmadog).*

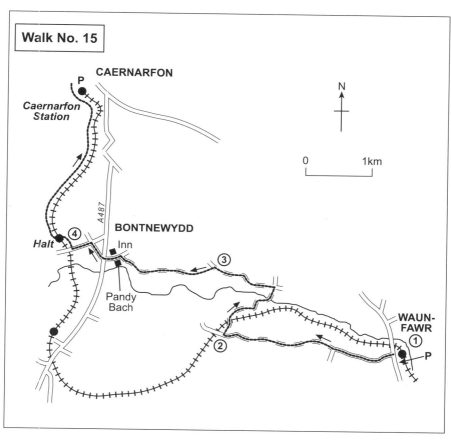

4. Just before passing under the railway bridge turn right up a path to the line. Cross the line and turn right along the track past Bontnewydd Halt. Follow the track for one and a half miles into Caernarfon.

Walk 16: Blaenau Ffestiniog to Tan-y-Bwlch via Dduallt

Ffestiniog Railway

Starting point: Tan-y-Bwlch Station car park signposted off the A496 at the Oakeley Arms.

Distance: 7 miles (11.3 kilometres) or 2.5 miles (4 kilometres) from Dduallt (see below)

Height gain: 820 feet (250 metres), or 160 feet (50 metres) from Dduallt

Relevant maps: Explorer OL18 (Harlech, Porthmadog and Bala), Landranger 115 (Snowdon) and 124 (Dolgellau)

Facilities: Car park, café and toilets at Tan-y-Bwlch and a wide range of facilities in Blaenau Ffestiniog.

Terrain: Mostly clear paths and tracks, some soft ground likely to be encountered. Modest climb to Dduallt. The route is fairly obvious except between Dolwen Cottage and Dduallt.

Local information: There is no road access to Dduallt Halt, so it is not practicable to do this as two separate walks. Slate spoil heaps loom large over Blaenau Ffestiniog which flourished in the 19th century after the Ffestiniog Railway was built. Over 4,000 men were employed here at the peak of production in the 1880s, the main line being completed in 1879. Llechwedd Slate Caverns and Gloddfa Ganol Slate Mine are now principally tourist features. Blaenau Ffestiniog may enjoy a revival in the near future as technological advances enable the slate spoil to be reconstituted as a building material.

Take the train from Tan-y-Bwlch to Blaenau Ffestiniog. *The shorter alternative is to leave the train at Dduallt and follow the walk from paragraph number 5 onwards.*

1. Turn left out of the station car park along the main road past the church and turn left to cross the footbridge over the railway line. Walk straight on, then bear left down the enclosed waymarked path parallel to Bryn Bowydd. Go through a kissing gate and

Pulling into Tan-y-Bwlch

descend more steeply along the clear path later undulating along the side of the valley. Pass through the ornamental gate in the wall ahead and, at the end of the path, bear right on a concreted track.

2. Turn right along the road for 80 metres and then turn left down a track over Afon Goddal. Fork right at a junction of tracks to pass Dolwen Cottage. 20 metres further on bear left along an initially faint path through a cleared forest plantation. The path is indicated by marker posts at intervals and becomes more obvious as it converges with the river below. Follow the path away from the river and then turn left at a junction to cross a footbridge over the river.

3. Walk straight on along the obvious path but, at a left-hand bend, go forward through a gate and woodland. At the end of this path turn right along a track. Turn left along a minor track immediately before reaching the restored longhouse, through kissing gates and past a bog called "The Mire".

*There are information boards alongside the tracks giving more
detailed information.*

4. Follow a track, bending left, and then turn right at the information board about oaks. Turn right alongside the river and cross
   the footbridge. Follow the clear path bending right uphill and
   bear left over a little stream into a conifer plantation. Continue
   climbing over rock outcrops and cross the ladder stile at the top
   end of the plantation. Walk by the wall to the right and eventually cross the ladder stile over this wall. Turn left up the faint
   track and then bear right up a clear stony track. Fork left at a
   junction of tracks and, after 25 metres, turn left up a minor track
   which converges with the original track bed of the Ffestiniog
   Railway at a ladder stile.

5. Cross the ladder stile on the right at the far end of Dduallt Halt
   (the ladder stile to the left, after a short detour, leads up to a
   viewpoint in the middle of the loop). Turn left alongside the line
   and, 40 metres after passing under a bridge, bear left by a large
   stone along a faint path (not the obvious path uphill). Keep
   roughly the same distance from the telephone wires initially
   between rock outcrops. Converge with and cross the railway
   track, then carry on in the same direction down to Dduallt
   Manor House.

   *This attractive and very solidly built house dates from about 1450.
   Oliver Cromwell used it as quarters in 1648 while his forces
   completed the defeat of the Royalists in Wales. It is now owned by
   the National Trust but is not open to the public.*

6. Go forward over a junction of tracks and after 10 metres turn
   right up the well-worn path. Cross the stile over the wire fence
   ahead and carry on down to a footbridge. Walk on alongside a
   fence to the right gradually converging with, and then beside the
   railway line.

7. Pass an isolated cottage at the station halt, Coed-y-bleiddiau,
   where the path starts to diverge from the railway. Cross a footbridge and later fork left to pass through the waymarked
   handgate. Follow the increasingly broad, clear track down

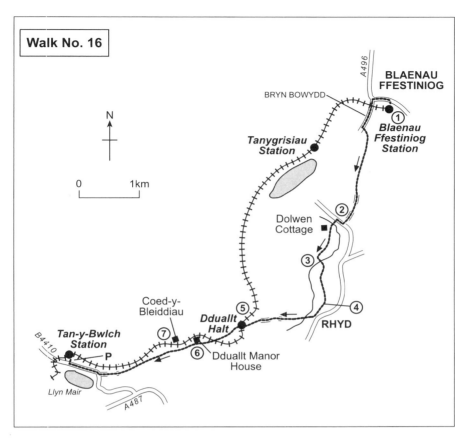

Walk No. 16

through a dense conifer plantation. Bear right at a junction and cross the footbridge over a stream, climbing briefly, before the descent to the road. Turn right alongside the lake, cross the footbridge at the far end of the car park and climb the stepped path to Tan-y-Bwlch Station.

Walk 17: Rhydyronen to Aberdovey

Cambrian Coast Line and Talyllyn Railway

Starting point: Aberdovey Station car park on the west side of town.

Distance: 7.5 miles (12.1 kilometres)

Height gain: 1570 feet (480 metres)

Relevant maps: Explorer OL 23 (Cadair Idris & Bala Lake), Landranger 135 (Aberystwyth & Machynlleth)

Facilities: Aberdovey and Tywyn including the Talyllyn Wharf Station.

Terrain: Mostly firm tracks, quiet lanes and a fairly clear route. A long gradual climb to the ridge and equally gradual descent into Happy Valley. The secondary climb out of Happy Valley is shorter, before the easy descent to Aberdovey.

Local information: Aberdovey (in Welsh, Aberdyfi, meaning mouth of the River Dyfi) is a compact seaside resort on the southern tip of the Snowdonia National Park. It is nevertheless blessed with two railway stations – Penhelig Station is on the east side of the town.

Take the Cambrian Coast Line from Aberdovey to Tywyn and then the Talyllyn narrow-guage from Tywyn Wharf to Rhydyronen, allowing 10 minutes to walk between stations in Tywyn. If time permits, the museum at Wharf Station is well worth a visit. The station provides a good backdrop for photos of the train; the bridge at the end of the halt at Rhydyronen is also a good vantage point.

1. Leave the station by way of the privet-lined avenue and turn right along the lane over the railway bridge. Follow the lane, bending left past Plas Coch and then gaining height very gradually. Walk straight on passing through a gate shortly after which the lane deteriorates to a stony track. Cross a stile beside a gate and almost immediately ford a stream. Go on up the increasingly steep track and cross the stile by another gate, where the ground is very soft, and later ford a stream. Carry on along the track which then levels off and cross a stile by a gate across the track.

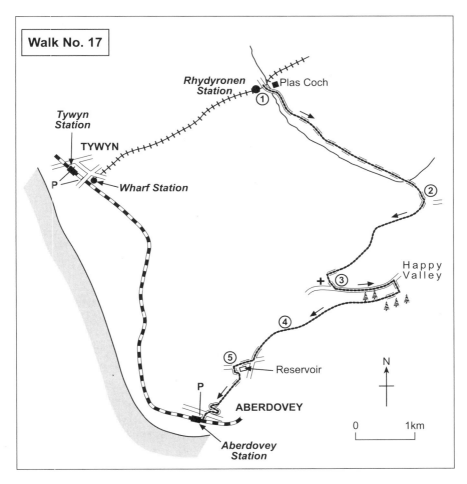

On a clear day, views from this point extend over Cardigan Bay to the Lleyn Peninsula and, later, south-west over the Dovey Valley and along the coast.

2.   Walk on for 35 metres and turn sharply right along the less distinct grassy track past a marker post. Walk straight on as the track becomes less clear still ascending gradually and crossing the stile by a gate across the track. Go straight on at a junction of tracks where there are extensive views to the south over Happy Valley, and commence the descent into the valley. The track is

joined by another, more distinct, from the right and descends more steeply bending left to a gate. Go through the gate and carry on down the track, again indistinct, gradually bending right. Pass through the left-hand of two adjacent gates. Follow the increasingly clear sunken track alongside the fence to the right. Continue the descent down the enclosed track and bear left along the farm track to the road in the valley, quite near to the chapel.

> *This is Happy Valley, known particularly for short walks from a car park higher up the valley to Bearded Lake (Llyn Bartog) and Carn March Arthur (alleged hoofmark of Arthur's steed). For those with a vivid imagination the outline of the lake shows the face of an old man, the reeds being his beard. The rock, legend would have us believe, bears the hoof print of King Arthur's horse after jumping the Dovey Estuary! It is an attractive spot and the view over the Estuary is well worth the short climb.*

3. Turn left along the road for a few hundred metres and then turn right along a surfaced track bearing left of holiday cottages. Cross the stile ahead and follow the stony track to a ford. Cross the footbridge to the right and turn right up the track. After a short steep climb the track climbs obliquely through and then above woodland. Go straight on at a junction of tracks just above the woodland where the main track bends left. 100 metres after passing through the next gate, and immediately after passing through a small embankment, fork right along the fainter track to contour across a large field.

> *Having completed the second climb of the day, the remainder of the walk is a pleasant descent into Aberdovey.*

4. Turn left through the gate in the top fence near the far corner and follow the clearer track by fences to the left and then to the right, and later enclosed. Cross an asphalt track and then follow the lane ahead. At a junction of lanes bear right down a stony track.

5. At the next junction turn left to pass around two sides of the reservoir. Carry on down this track descending towards Aberdovey. Walk straight on down an enclosed grassy track at a

'Douglas' (disguised as Duncan in the Reverend Awdry's famous railway books)

left-hand bend. Continue the descent above houses as the track deteriorates to a path. Cross a ladder stile to a junction of roads, of which one is Maesnewydd. Turn right down the narrow lane bending left then sharply right to the main road. Bear left across the road to the station car park.

Walk 18: Llanrwst to Betws-y-Coed

Conwy Valley Line

Starting point: Any one of three car parks in Betws-y-Coed, the most convenient being opposite the railway station.

Distance: 8 miles (12.9 kilometres)

Height gain: 1200 feet (360 metres)

Relevant maps: Explorer OL17 (Snowdon/Conwy Valley), Landranger 115 (Snowdon)

Facilities: Good range in both Betws-y-Coed and Llanrwst.

Terrain: Mainly firm tracks interspersed with forest paths, fields and lanes. Principal ascent, steep at times, near the start of the walk and short steep descent to the Miners' Bridge. The route is quite clear except for the section between St Rhychwyn's Church and Castell y Gwynt.

Local information: A short detour from the square in Llanrwst down Church Street leads past the old almshouses to St Grwst Church and Gwydyr Chapel. The latter dating from 1633 and elaborately decorated was the memorial chapel of the influential Wynn family and also houses a stone coffin said to be that of Llywelyn the Great (died 1420). The family enlarged Gwydyr Castle and built Gwydyr Uchaf Chapel near the castle.

Take the train from Betws-y-Coed to Llanrwst (the principal station being the first stop from Betws-y-Coed, ***not*** the next station, Llanrwst North).

1. Turn left out of the station to cross the bridge over the line. Walk straight on where the major road swings left down to the square and centre of Llanrwst. Turn left along the A470 and then turn right across the bridge over the River Conwy, still quite narrow at this point.

    This bridge was the first crossing of the river in the Conwy Valley and the 15th-century building on the opposite side of the river was originally the courthouse. The stone circle is modern, commemorating the Eisteddford of 1951. The road ahead leads to Gwydir Castle and Chapel (both open to the public).

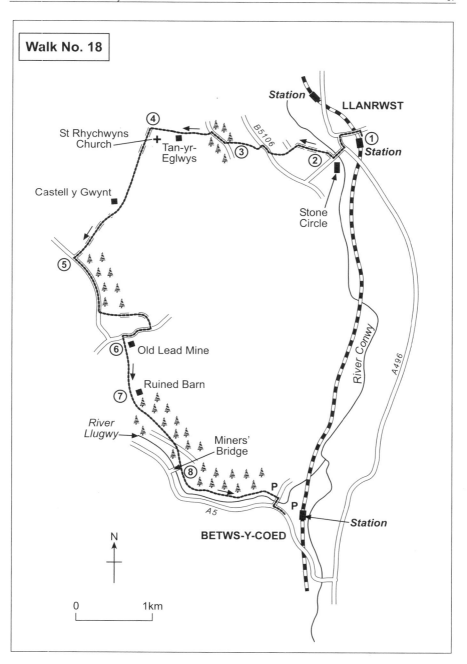

Walk No. 18

Station LLANRWST

B5106

① Station

St Rhychwyns Church

④

Tan-yr-Eglwys

③

②

Castell y Gwynt

Stone Circle

⑤

River Conwy

A496

⑥ Old Lead Mine

Ruined Barn

⑦

River Llugwy

Miners' Bridge

⑧

P

P

A5

Station

BETWS-Y-COED

N

0 1km

2. 40 metres from the bridge, turn right along an enclosed track. Where this track bends sharply right cross the stile ahead and bear right alongside the fence to reach a road. Turn right along this road for about 100 metres and then turn left up an enclosed path. Cross the stile and bear right to pass through the gap in a stone wall. Turn right, through the handgate in a new wire fence, alongside the wall. Go through the kissing gate in the top corner of the field, cross a ladder stile and track to follow the well-worn path into woodland. Climb increasingly steeply, forking left at a junction, later crossing a footbridge, where the path is stepped, up to a lane.

3. Turn right up this lane and turn sharply left up a waymarked track at the top edge of woodland by a small bridge. Cross a ladder stile to follow the increasingly clear and partly enclosed track. Walk on through a field gate over a field to join another track to a farm. Approaching the farm, Tan-yr-Eglwys, bear left at the junction of tracks and then turn right up the stepped path opposite the back corner of the farmhouse. Go through a kissing gate and bear left to pass through another kissing gate by a cottage. Bear left up towards the church and pass through yet another kissing gate in the top fence of the field. Turn left to the lichgate of a lovely unspoilt church.

> *This is the 11th-century church of St Rhychwyn, said to be the church of Llewellyn the Great. The lichgate bears the date 1462, altered from 1762, whilst the ancient font is probably the oldest feature of the church.*

4. Turn left out of the lichgate and go through the kissing gate in the top corner of the field. Walk straight on along the track and subsequently an enclosed path. Cross a ladder stile, bear left for 20 metres and then turn right as indicated by the waymarker on the rocky ground. Follow the clear winding path through a plantation. Leave the trees by way of a ladder stile over the boundary wall and go up the faint grassy track, winding in roughly the same direction, towards the crest of the far hill. After about 200 metres the track becomes more obvious and the next ladder stile, by a gate, can be seen ahead. Cross the ladder stile and

The memorable 11th-century St. Rhychwyn's Church

carry on along the initially well-worn path and then straight on alongside a dilapidated wall to the right. Go over the crest of the hill as a small lake comes into view below. Carry on towards this lake and go through the gate ahead to join a faint grassy track which leads across the frontage of Castell y Gwynt. Follow the clear track through old mine-workings and around a cluster of buildings to reach a lane.

5. Turn left up the lane, climbing steeply, ignoring the finger post on the left into dense forestry. About 80 metres after passing enclosed mine-workings to the left, where the lane is fairly level, and 30 metres before reaching a gate on the right turn left up the initially faint path (not waymarked). This fairly straight path soon becomes reassuringly distinct, rising gradually to a forest track. Cross this track and follow the track ahead to a T-junction and turn right. Pass a cottage and go straight on at the nearby junction. At the end of the track turn right and, almost immediately, turn right again along a lane to the remains of a lead mine.

Cyffty Lead Mine was established in the 1850s. The area has been landscaped and there are information boards about the history of the site.

6. Bear left down the stony path through the site and turn left before reaching the lane again, cross a ladder stile and the field ahead. Cross the ladder stile at a junction of stone walls, bear right and right again down a track as indicated by marker posts. Cross another ladder stile and follow the track between a ruined outbuilding and marker post. Descend past an orphan ladder stile in the far corner of a field and bear left by a fence. Nearing the bottom of the field turn right to cross the ladder stile in the fence ahead and turn left along a track into forestry by way of another stile. Turn right at a T-junction of tracks, leave the woodland by way of a stile and carry on along the less obvious track bending left to a junction by a ruined barn.

7. Go along the stony track past the barn for 20 metres and bear right at a marker post down a path by a stone wall. Bear right at the end of the wall to another wall and bear left to cross a ladder stile into woodland. Descend steeply initially before the path broadens and sweeps down the hillside. Cross a track and a lane, where the path again becomes steep briefly, descending towards the miners' bridge.

8. Before reaching the bridge, turn left by the fence down the riverside path to Betws-y-Coed. Pass through the car park, turn right over the bridge, then turn left down the A5 into the centre and other car parks by the station.

Walk 19: Snowdon Ranger Youth Hostel to Waunfawr

Welsh Highland Railway (Caernarfon)

Starting point: Waunfawr Station car park alongside the A4085 south of the village

Distance: 8 miles (12.9 kilometres)

Height gain: 1400 feet (430 metres)

Relevant maps: Explorer OL17 (Snowdon & Conwy Valley) Landranger 115 (Snowdon)

Facilities: Toilets and inn by Waunfawr station car park. Full facilities in Caernarfon.

Terrain: Easy route finding along very obvious, firm tracks and paths. A steep climb for the first mile, gentle descent for two miles, further short climb and long gradual descent.

Take the train along the new extension of track to the halt above the Snowdon Ranger Youth Hostel. Another very obvious option provided by this extension to Rhyd Ddu is to park at the car park opposite the Youth Hostel and take the train to Rhyd Ddu. Climb the Rhyd Ddu Path to the summit of Snowdon and descend by way of the Snowdon Ranger Path. Further extension of the line opens up opportunities for strenuous linear walks utilising the Rhyd Ddu and Watkin paths on Snowdon, and other paths over Moel Hebog and Cnicht.

1.   Walk down the platform back towards Waunfawr and then turn right up the track crossing the line (the Snowdon Ranger Path). Pass a cottage with a waterwheel fixed to the wall, and fork right as indicated by the arrow on the boulder. Carry on up the obvious path soon climbing more steeply. Go on through a gate before zigzagging up the mountainside. Pass through the gap in a stone wall and, about 200 metres further on, turn sharply uphill at a marker post signed to Llanberis, leaving the Snowdon

'Millennium' at Castell Cidwm

Ranger Path (this marker post is some 400 metres before the next gate across the Snowdon Ranger Path).

2. Climb steeply up the bank where the path is not clear. After about 200 metres pass a simple bench sheltered between two rocky outcrops where the path is quite distinct. Follow the increasingly clear path, as the gradient eases, heading towards the pass hopefully now in view ahead. Cross two ladder stiles to reach the high point which is nearly halfway up Snowdon. Descend gradually along the very clear stony path in the direction of Llanberis.

> *After nearly a mile, the scarred hillside of the Dinorwic Quarries above Llanberis comes into view. Llanberis is home to the Snowdon Mountain Railway, Britain's only rack and pinion railway, and engines may well be sighted on the opposite hillside. The railway, and some of the steam engines, date from 1896. The line is 4½ miles long and the average gradient 1:7.8.*

3. Continue walking down the improved path, which evolves into

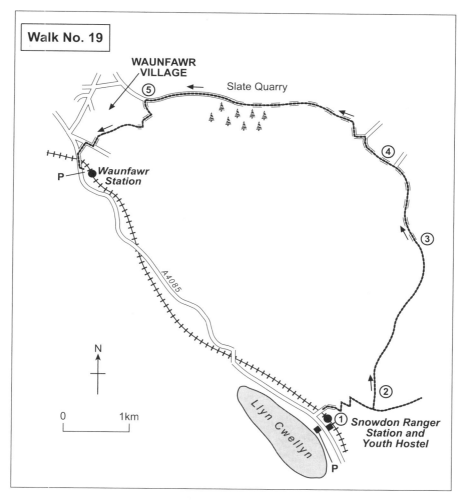

Walk No. 19

WAUNFAWR VILLAGE

Slate Quarry

⑤

P — **Waunfawr Station**

A4085

N

0   1km

④

③

②

① **Snowdon Ranger Station and Youth Hostel**

Llyn Cwellyn

P

a track on passing a cottage. Go through a gate and over the adjacent bridge. At a junction of tracks go straight on by way of a ladder stile up the rougher track.

4. Climb briefly before crossing another ladder stile where the track deteriorates to a level path. Pass through a gate and turn left at the T-junction up a partly surfaced track which bends sharply right by a ruined building. Climb steeply to cross the ladder stile on the skyline and follow the stony track bending left near the wall, as the gradient eases. Cross a further ladder stile and follow the track, now downhill, between a conifer plantation and slate spoil. This track evolves into a surfaced lane which bends right descending increasingly steeply.

This is part of the Four Valleys long-distance trail which runs from Bethesda in the Ogwen Valley, through Llanberis in the Padarn Valley, Waunfawr in the Gwyrfai Valley and, finally, through the Nantlle Valley to Penygroes. The trail provides a well waymarked route from the lane into Waunfawr which would otherwise be difficult to follow. The route is nevertheless fully described below.

5. Turn left down a track where a finger post is signed "Waunfawr ¾ mile" and displaying the trail motif. Cross the footbridge over a stream, go through a gate and turn right alongside the stream. Cross the stone stile by a gate and follow the track bending left and right. Leave the track at a marker post to contour along the bottom edge of two fields by way of a handgate and footbridge. Bear left alongside a stone wall and continue in the same direction through a gap in a stone wall ahead, briefly down a surfaced track and through two kissing gates. Bear right to ford a stream and pass a marker post along the bottom edge of a field. Go through another kissing gate and bear left alongside a stone wall through a further kissing gate to join an enclosed path. Bear right across a track and at the end of the enclosed path turn right along a lane. After 100 metres turn left down another enclosed path to the road. Turn left along the A4085 back to the car park.

Walk 20: Nant Gwernol to Morfa Mawddach

Cambrian Coast Line and Talyllyn Railway

Starting point: Morfa Mawddach station, signposted down a lane off the A493 Dolgellau to Tywyn road.

Distance: 8 miles (12.9 kilometres)

Height gain: 1480 feet (450 metres)

Relevant maps: Explorer OL23 (Cadair Idris & Bala Lake), Landranger 124 (Dolgellau) and 135 (Aberystwyth & Machynlleth)

Facilities: Toilet, inn and café in Abergynolwyn en route. Facilities in Fairbourne and Dolgellau.

Terrain: Firm tracks and short stretch of soft path descending through forestry plantation. Route finding quite easy, single steep ascent and the part of the descent mentioned above is fairly steep.

Take the Cambrian Coast train from Morfa Mawddach to Tywyn. Cross the station car park and turn right along the road to Wharf Station (allow 10 minutes) and take the Talyllyn train to the end of the line at Nant Gwernol.

1. Go along the level path at the end of the line across the footbridge and follow the obvious path down the gorge. Carry on along the path which eventually bears right to a lane, and turn left into Abergynolwyn.

2. Turn left along the main road for 75 metres and turn right, between the playground and stream, down a track. Turn left across the footbridge over the stream and go along the partly paved path. Bear right by cottages, climb steps and go straight on along the well-used path. Cross a ladder stile and contour along the side of the valley over another two stiles. Bear left past a marker post above the landslip, then fork right to follow the riverside path, which develops into an increasingly clear track.

'Sir Haydn' crossing the forest track a short distance above Abergynolwyn Station

Carry on past the frontage of Rhiwlas and turn right over the bridge along the lane.

3. Approaching a phone box, turn left down another lane. Go straight on at the next junction by a farm and, at the end of the lane, cross the bridge over a stream. Carry on up the obvious track but soon turn left over a ladder stile by a finger post, up the clear grassy track. Follow this track winding uphill and over two stiles. Bear right, still climbing the grassy track, to pass above conifer plantations and over two ladder stiles. A fence on the left then joins the track, at a right-hand bend. Cross the ladder stile at the top corner of the fencing and continue, bearing right at a marker post. Converge with and eventually join a stony track as another ladder stile appears ahead. About 150 metres beyond this stile bear right at a marker post, along a minor track which soon becomes clearer as the gradient eases. Carry on along this track, climb a ladder stile, converge with the stone wall to the right and pass through two gates close together. Cross a ladder stile a short distance further on to join a stony track climbing

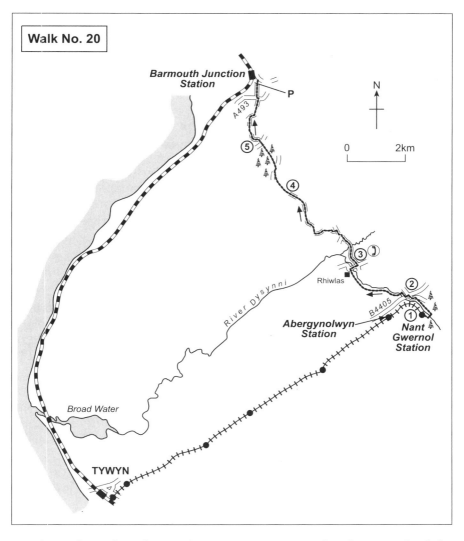

from the right. The track soon converges with a fence to the left. Go through the handgate in this fence (or climb the adjacent ladder stile!)

The slab of slate by the gate is marked as a trig point and also bears the initials WWEW. At this point looking back there is a good view of the peak of Cadair Idris.

4. Follow a narrow, but fairly clear, path bending right to contour across the shoulder of the hill and eventually converge with a track climbing from the left, by woodland. Bear right along this track and about 125 metres after passing through a gate, turn left down the waymarked track into the forestry. Go straight across a clearing with a grassy mound covered in stones, leaving the track. Descend steeply along a broad path, crossing two tracks to emerge from the forestry at a junction of tracks.

5. Go down the track opposite, through the kissing gate, and to the right of a large house. Bear right down the enclosed track and bear right at ensuing junctions to carry on down the major track. Pass through the kissing gate beside the gate across the track which soon bends sharply left to another junction indicated by a marker post. Turn sharply right along a fairly level track and go over two ladder stiles.

Bear left to converge with the track on the left then turn right down a path rather than following the track through a gateway. Cross two ladder stiles between which the path is enclosed and then carry on across a track to pass through the kissing gate on the right. Follow the path bending left steeply downhill and turn right over the ladder stile in the bottom fence. Go down to the track and turn left, then soon bear right across a junction to go through a handgate. Follow the enclosed path to the A493 and turn left. After 75 metres turn right opposite the war memorial down to the station, as signposted.

Walk 21: Dolwyddelan to Betws-y-Coed

Conwy Valley Line

Starting point: Two car parks opposite Betws-y-Coed Station and another at the top end of village passed at the end of the walk.

Distance: 8.5 miles (13.7 kilometres)

Height gain: 620 feet (190 metres)

Relevant maps: Explorer OL17 (Snowdon/Conwy Valley) and OL18 (Harlech, Porthmadog and Bala), Landranger 115 (Snowdon)

Facilities: Inn, café and toilets in Dolwyddelan, wide range of facilities in Betws-y-Coed.

Terrain: Track, country lane and riverside path. Generally firm ground and a short steep climb at the start. Route finding is generally easy, but care required at the junctions of forest tracks where the ground is otherwise featureless.

Local information: Betws-y-Coed is the eastern gateway to Snowdonia, access being limited by the few crossings of the River Conwy. It is extremely popular in peak season both as a holiday centre and for refreshment en route to or from the National Park. The famous cast-iron Waterloo Bridge constructed by Thomas Telford in 1815 carries the A5 over the river. There are motor and railway museums and, surrounding the village, various features of interest. Walks in the area include some of these features.

Take the train from Betws-y-Coed to Dolwyddelan.

1. Turn left out of the station car park and then right at the T-junction across the river towards the centre of the village.

    St Gwydellan's Church is hidden amongst trees on the left of the lane. It was built in the late 16th century by the owner of Dolwyddelan Castle who, at that time, also owned Gwydir Castle.

2. Cross the main road and go straight up the lane ahead. Turn right at the T-junction and bear left over a ladder stile to cross

the next ladder stile on the other side of the field. Bear right to contour across a field by a fence and join a track into the forest.

3. Turn left at the T-junction uphill and, as the track levels out, fork left along the major track soon crossing a river by way of a concrete bridge. Cross another similar bridge over the same river after about a half-mile. Pass a track on the right after about 50 metres and, after another 50 metres, bear right at another junction, waymarked to Capel Curig (the track to the left leads to Moel Siabod). Go straight on at the next junction but after a further 80 metres fork right along the minor grassy track soon leaving the forest by way of a ladder stile.

4. Carry on along the very obvious track, crossing another ladder stile, and straight on at the intersection where the descent commences. At the bottom of the track soon after crossing a ladder stile, turn right along the lane for about a mile to the A5. Turn left over the bridge by the Ugly House.

   The Ugly House (Ty Hyll) is a small cottage built of massive boulders. The roughly-built chimney is a good example of 'freeholding': in the Middle Ages, the freehold right to common land

The Ugly House

could be established if a prospective freeholder could build a rough house (like Ty Hyll) overnight and have smoke coming out of the chimney by dawn.

5. Turn right down steps to join the riverside path. Walk downstream and then away from the river to join a track, where there is a marker post. Fork right at the next marker post and after 50 metres bear left at a junction of paths to pass above Swallow Falls. Detour down steps to the viewing platform for a clearer view of the falls.

6. Carry on down the obvious path and at a junction go straight on, signposted to Betws-y-Coed. Cross a footbridge and bear right at

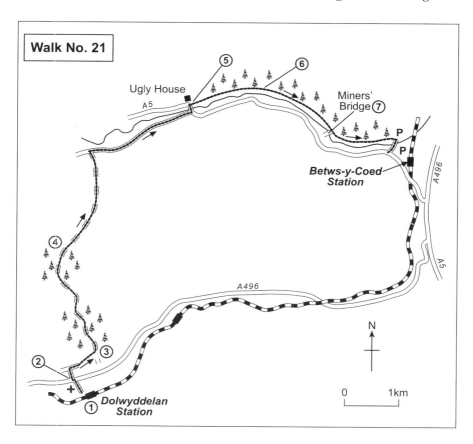

a junction of paths. After 50 metres fork left along a fairly level path through trees. Pass through a dilapidated stone wall and climb briefly. Turn right at the next junction of paths as indicated by a finger post and cross a footbridge where the path levels out again. Bear right along a lane and bear right downhill at the next marker post. Follow the path between the lane and river descending to the miners' bridge.

7. Go straight on down the riverside path staying on the same side of the river to a car park. Turn right over the stone bridge and turn left down the A5 to the centre of Betws-y-Coed.

Walk 22: Conwy to Penmaenmawr

Chester – Holyhead Line

Starting point: Car park opposite Penmaenmawr Station

Distance: 8.5 miles (13.7 kilometres)

Height gain: 1200 feet (370 metres)

Relevant maps: Explorer OL17 (Snowdon & Conwy Valley), Landranger 115 (Snowdon)

Facilities: Toilets in car park, other facilities in the centre of town. Wide range of facilities in Conwy.

Terrain: Firm tracks/paths, and latterly a country lane. Gradual ascent but steeper descent. Generally well waymarked except for a short distance descending Conwy Mountain to the Sychnant Pass. Route finding is quite clear except on Conwy Mountain where there are numerous paths, which are not always rights of way.

Take the train from Penmaenmawr to Conwy.

Conwy is a World Heritage Site and the jewel in the crown of Snowdonia. Edward I built the castle and fortified the town in 1283-7. Within the walls, which are the best example standing in Britain, are Plas Mawr (Elizabethan town house), Aberconwy House (only remaining medieval house), and St Mary and All Saints' Church (13th century). Outside the walls is the first river crossing of the River Conwy at this point: Telford's bridge, which dates from 1826. Beside this is Robert Stephenson's railway bridge of 1848. Nowadays most traffic uses the tunnel carrying the A55 by-passing Conwy but the railway still goes through the middle of the town. Llandudno and the Great Orme, on the other side of the estuary, also have features of interest to the visitor.

1. Turn right out of Conwy Station and pass the visitors centre. Turn left down Castle Street and then turn right down High Street through the old wall. Turn left along the edge of the harbour and again pass through the town walls. After 40 metres, turn right to join an enclosed path along the shoreline, joining the North Wales Path.

Train coming into Conwy Station inside the medieval walls

2. Turn left on reaching a road to pass Aberconwy School and cross the old A55 coast road by the tollhouse. Walk straight on up the track opposite, crossing the footbridge over the railway line. At the end of this track bear right up a lane. At the top of the lane fork right as indicated to climb the ladder stile ahead. Carry on up the steep well-worn path, crossing another path. Bear left at a junction along a more level path, still following signs for the North Wales Path. (A short detour up the path to the right leads to a splendid view over the estuary and the Great Orme.)

3. Bear left at another junction of paths and almost immediately cross a track, still ascending gradually. (The alternative path to the right which is higher up the ridge provides better views but is the more energetic route. It is not waymarked but eventually converges with the path described.) After a short descent bear right away from the sandy track below. Bear right as indicated by marker posts at further junctions of paths. (The alternative path mentioned above drops down to the long distance path where there is another superb view of the Great Orme.) Fork left

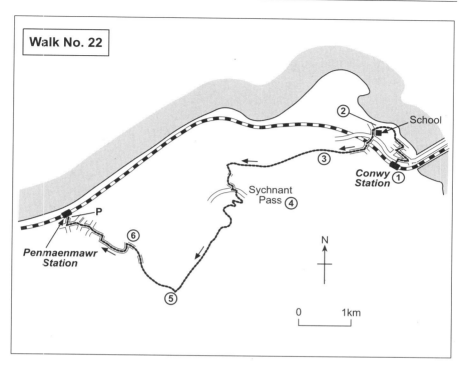

at the next junction of paths and follow the clear grassy path to a junction of stony tracks. Go straight on as indicated, initially uphill, then descend to cross a farm track. Again ascend briefly then join a track which descends to the road at the top of the Sychnant Pass ('dry ravine' in Welsh).

4. Bear left across the road through a gate and along the clear path. At the next junction of paths turn sharply right uphill. Follow the major path bending left then right after which Anglesey and Puffin Island come into view. Carry on up the winding path passing beneath overhead cables ignoring the path to the right. Cross the ladder stile by a gate ahead and walk down the obvious track. Fork left under overhead cables and then fork right under the same cables to carry on alongside the stone wall. Diverge from the wall along a clearer path, contouring across the hillside and ignoring tracks bending left uphill. Turn right at a ruined farmstead.

5. Bear left at the corner of the boundary wall and cross the foot-bridge and ladder stile in the gully below. Climb the clear path away from the stream and then bear right at a fork in the paths towards a ladder stile and finger post, leaving the North Wales Path. Cross the ladder stile and follow the clear path diverging from the wall. Join a clear stony track soon starting the fairly steep descent towards Penmaenmawr, which comes into view below.

6. Follow the track bending sharply left (the path ahead between stone pillars is called the Jubilee Path) where it becomes a lane. Go straight on at several road junctions towards the centre of town and then turn left at a T junction. Bear left at the next T-junction up the main street and turn right at crossroads down to the station.

Walk 23: Llanfairfechan to Bangor

Chester – Holyhead Line

Starting point: Station car park at Bangor

Distance: 9 miles (14.5 kilometres)

Height gain: 400 feet (120 metres)

Relevant maps: Explorer OL17 (Snowdon & Conwy Valley) Landranger 115 (Snowdon)

Facilities: Inns, hotels and cafes in Llanfairfechan and a wide range of facilities in Bangor. Toilets near to both stations.

Terrain: Mostly flat sandy ground, hilly on the outskirts of Bangor, utilising quiet lanes and paths. The sandy ground drains quickly but may be soft when dry making the walking more difficult. Fairly obvious route.

Local information: Bangor is a university town with a thriving high street. The railway station is sited near one end of the high street whilst at the other end is the much restored cathedral, dating from the 12th to 16th centuries, and museum/art gallery. The renovated Victorian Pier, 1550 feet long, extends more than half-way across the Menai Strait to Anglesey, and is now one of the best preserved in the country. Nearby highlights include Edward I's Beaumaris Castle, the beautiful Menai Strait with Telford's graceful road bridge of 1826 and Robert Stephenson's railway bridge of 1850 (the latter much restored and now also the principal road crossing).

Take the train from Bangor to Llanfairfechan (request stop). The route immediately takes walkers away from Llanfairfechan, where the railway briefly attracted holidaymakers to its sheltered situation. Birdwatchers, no doubt carrying binoculars, will linger on this walk using the numerous hides provided.

1. Turn right out of the station and then turn left through the recreation ground to the pond. Turn left along the surfaced path and go through a gate where there is the first of many information boards.

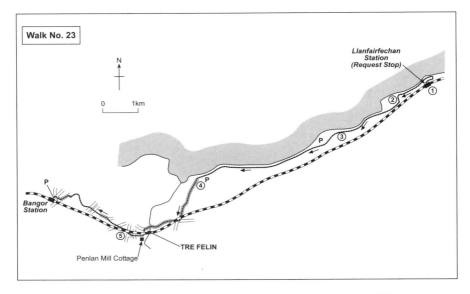

This board provides information about the Glan y Mor Elias nature reserve, one of a chain of such reserves along this stretch of coast, which is sheltered to some extent by Anglesey. Some of the reserves also have very useful picnic tables.

2.   Carry on along the path on an embankment bending away from the shore and straight on at a junction of embankments. Bear right alongside the railway line and cross a bridge by another information board. Bear right to join the path along the foreshore initially outside the boundary fence of Morfa Madryn nature reserve.

3.   After walking for about one mile, cross the footbridge over a stream that emerges from the nearby woodland and join the enclosed track along the edge of the foreshore. Go through two kissing gates and bear left to a junction of tracks where there is a finger post. Bear right along the track between the wall and car park (where there is an information board relating to the Morfa Aber nature reserve). Follow a stony track which deteriorates to the sandy foreshore . Later join another track before being forced onto the sand again.

Penrhyn Castle from the foreshore

Ahead, on the wooded peninsula ('penrhyn' in Welsh), is Penrhyn Castle. This Neo-Norman fortified manor house dates from the early 1800s, built by the owner of slate quarries at Bethesda and Jamaican sugar plantations. The furnishings remain in the property, now in the care of the National Trust, and outbuildings house an Industrial Railway Museum and Doll Collection.

4. A good half-mile further on, bear left through a car park and down the lane past the Spinnies and Traeth Lafan nature reserves. Cross the railway line and turn right at a T-junction, soon crossing the railway line again. Cross a river and turn left down Tre Felin, at the bottom of which turn right past terraced houses. Go under the railway line, turn right and climb past Penlan Mill Cottage. Continue alongside the line up a path to the road. Cross this road and go up the road opposite. Soon turn right up a path as indicated by a finger post, cross the major road and go through the kissing gate opposite.

5. Go along the enclosed path and cross a lane by way of two kissing gates. Follow the obvious path across a track, now with the

railway line to the left. Bear left down the road through an industrial estate, at the bottom of which cross a track and the footbridge over a stream. Fork left up a clear path, go forward through a housing estate and continue up the obvious enclosed path ahead. Cross another path and, as the path levels out, ignore gates providing access to the golf course on both sides of the path. At the next junction of paths near to the top of the hill bear left between dilapidated stone walls. Descend rapidly into Bangor and turn right down a lane to the high street. Turn left and then fork right up Holyhead Road to the railway station.

Walk 24: Dyffryn Ardudwy to Barmouth

Cambrian Coast Line

Starting point: Barmouth Station, on the Cambrian Coast Line.

Distance: 9 miles (14.5 kilometres)

Height gain: 1450 feet (440 metres)

Relevant maps: Explorer OL18 (Harlech, Porthmadog and Bala) and OL23(Cadair Idris & Bala Lake), Landranger 124 (Dolgellau)

Facilities: Wide range in Barmouth. Large pay and display car park within sight of the station.

Terrain: Largely firm tracks but some field paths where the ground is sometimes soft. Long and mostly gradual climb for the first half of the walk. The route as far as Pontfadog is fairly complex.

Local information: Barmouth is an old seaside resort which can still get very crowded in the peak summer season. This is not enough, however, to maintain prosperity and many Victorian slate buildings in the centre are showing the absence of maintenance. There is a lifeboat museum on the quay, a local museum in a medieval house (Ty Gwyn) and an unusual circular lockup (Ty Crwn); both of the latter open for limited hours in the summer.

Take the train from Barmouth to Dyffryn Ardudwy.

1. Cross the railway line and walk up the lane. Turn right at the crossroads along a narrow lane past a cottage, Pentre Bach. Bear right along the main road, A493, and turn left through a handgate up an enclosed path signposted to "Dyffryn Burial Chamber".

    This Neolithic communal burial ground is renowned as the most significant pre-Christian site in Snowdonia, dating from 5,000 years ago. There are two long barrows, both of which have been stripped of the mound with which they would originally have been covered. It is, of course, a National Monument and entry to the site is free.

Dyffryn Burial Chamber, passed at the start of the walk

2. Walk up the path outside the enclosure and through a handgate.
    Bear right as waymarked to pass between two poles carrying
    overhead cables. Bear right past the top corner of a wall along a
    path through woodland. Cross the first of the substantial stone
    stiles in the vicinity and walk alongside the wall to the left. Bear
    right at the marker post in the second field to pass through the
    gate in the wall ahead at the bottom end of the field. Go up the
    track on the other side of the lane, then bear right at the end of
    farm outbuildings to go through the gate in the bottom corner of
    the field. Walk alongside the wall to the left, cross a stone stile
    and go forward, now with a wall to the right. Climb a stile and
    turn right, cross another stile and turn left up a surfaced track.

3. Where the track turns left walk straight on into woods, cross a
    footbridge, immediately fork right and then turn right at a
    T-junction of tracks. Subsequently bear right along the major
    path and turn left at the next junction up a very straight track for
    over half a mile up a lovely wooded gorge, and later alongside
    the river. Turn right along the metalled track, past the cottage
    "Lletty Lloegr", over Pontfadog then bending left uphill again.

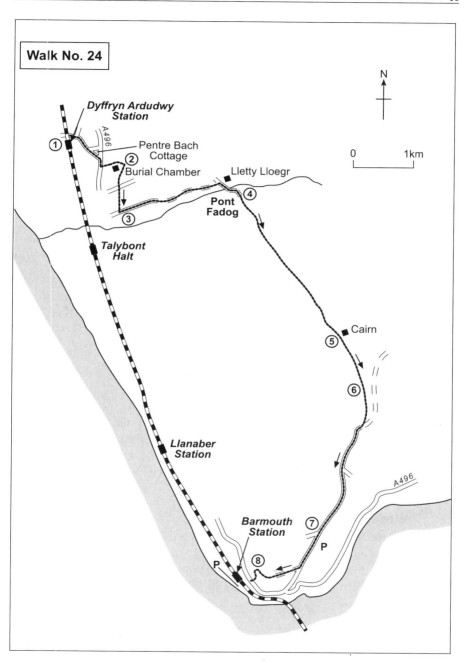

Walk No. 24

N

Dyffryn Ardudwy Station
① A496
Pentre Bach Cottage
②
■ Burial Chamber
Lletty Lloegr ■
Pont Fadog
④
③
Talybont Halt

0 _____ 1km

■ Cairn
⑤
⑥

Llanaber Station

A496

Barmouth Station ⑦
P
P
⑧
P

A stone on the parapet dates the bridge from 1762. It was probably an important junction of drove roads; the name of the cottage translates to 'English shelter' suggesting that it provided overnight accommodation for the drovers.

4. Go through the gate ahead and turn right between stone walls. Go forward along the minor track by the wall to the right. After 150 metres at a junction of tracks bear left uphill away from the wall past a white marker post. Cross the ladder stile by the gate in the top right-hand corner of the field. Walk straight on up the track past another white post to cross another ladder stile by a gate and carry on by a wall/fence to the right. Climb a ladder stile in a sheepfold and continue in the same direction diverging from the wall to the right. Pass through the gate in the top corner of the field and follow the obvious track to a cairn by a gate which is the high point of this walk.

    At this point the walk leaves the old drove road, which bends left to the west and descends into the top end of the Mawddach Estuary at Bontddu.

5. Go through the gate and bear right down the waymarked path then bear left of a ruin to go through the gate in the corner of the wall ahead. Bear right downhill keeping in sight of the wall to the right. Pass through the gap in another wall ahead and cross the stile in the fence on the other side of this wall. Descend gradually to the wall below, pass through the gate in this wall and carry on down the track by the wall. Follow the now faint track diverging from a complex of walls to go through the gate at the junction of a fence and a wall.

6. Follow the clearer track parallel to the wall on the right past the remains of a stone circle. Converge with, and bear right along, a stony track. Then, above a farm, turn right down a lane. This lane, in about one and half miles, leads down into Barmouth but the following route leaves the lane after one mile.

7. Keep left at a junction of lanes downhill past the car park. Just after this junction there is a signposted detour (The Panorama Walk) to the left to a well-known viewpoint over the Barmouth

Estuary. Bear right up the second driveway past the junction of lanes towards Gorllwyn Fach, and turn right up steps before entering the private grounds of the house. Walk alongside the boundary fence to the left and turn left down an enclosed track. Bear right past houses and, as the main track bends left into Cae Fador, go straight on along the minor grassy track. Carry on through a handgate climbing briefly along the edge of Dinas Oleu.

This was the first property acquired by The National Trust after it was established in 1895. It was donated by Mrs Fanny Talbot, a local philanthropist inspired by the work of John Ruskin and his Guild of St George in the formation of 'ideal' rural communities. Mrs Talbot donated several cottages on Dinas Oleu for the creation of such a community and one of the tenants was Auguste Guyard, a refugee from France who had been involved in a similar social experiment in his homeland. He was a well-respected local figure who died in 1883. You can follow a short path to his burial place, "Frenchman's Grave", from where there is a fine view over Barmouth.

8. Descend the obvious steep, winding path into the centre of Barmouth.

Walk 25: Fairbourne to Barmouth

Fairbourne and Barmouth Steam Railway or Cambrian Coast Line

Starting point: Large car park on the sea side of the railway, diagonally opposite Barmouth Station.

Distance: 9.5 miles (15.3 kilometres)

Height gain: 1280 feet (390 metres)

Relevant maps: Explorer OL23 (Cadair Idris & Bala Lake), Landranger 124 (Dolgellau)

Facilities: Barmouth and, to a limited extent, Fairbourne. Large pay and display car park within sight of the railway station in Barmouth, and a short walk from the ferry at the opposite end of the car park.

Terrain: Tracks, paths and quiet lanes, generally firm ground. Most of the climbing is in the first two miles and there are several short energetic climbs in the first mile. There is a fairly short steep descent in a lovely wooded gorge. The last two miles are along a disused railway track bed and walkway over the Barmouth Bridge (small toll payable). The route finding is not always easy during the climb, where there are numerous junctions of paths to negotiate. The rest of the walk is easy to follow.

Local information: An old town with a harbour, Barmouth (the Welsh name is 'Abermaw') was a very popular Victorian seaside resort with a superb sandy beach. It retained its popularity well into the 20th century but many of the imposing slate built buildings are now showing the absence of maintenance. A four-acre plot on the cliffs above, Dinas Oleu, was the first property gifted to the National Trust in 1895. Llanaber church, two miles to the north, dates from the 13th century and has some surprisingly elaborate stonework for a simple village church of this vintage.

Ideally, take the ferry (April-September only; not Tuesdays and subject to tides and the weather) and Fairbourne miniature steam railway from the other side of the estuary to Fairbourne. Alternatively, take the Cambrian Coast Line train from Barmouth to Fairbourne, where the two stations are close together.

'Southern' by the ferry which crosses from Barmouth

1. Go over the Cambrian Coast Line level crossing and walk up to the A493. Turn right along the road and turn left opposite the garage up Ffordd yr Ysgol. After 70 metres turn right at a finger post up the enclosed path at the edge of the school playing field. Carry on up the obvious path through a kissing gate and handgate then turn right along a track passing between houses. Turn left through the farmyard and go straight on up a grassy waymarked track below the farm buildings. Fork right at a junction of tracks, initially level then down to a surfaced drive.

2. Turn left and, immediately before reaching Panteinion Hall, turn sharply right up a waymarked gated track. Pass through a kissing gate and after 50 metres go straight on at a junction of tracks. After following this track for about a quarter-mile, increasingly uphill, fork right at a junction of tracks as indicated by a marker post. Climb this track bending sharply right and go through the kissing gate beside the field gate. Almost immediately, fork left at the next junction of tracks to pass above a small stone cottage. Carry on along the principal track, later between

dry stone walls, and then past a large isolated house to a finger post at the edge of a conifer plantation.

3. Bear left over the metalled track along a grassy track through the conifers. Continue climbing gently after crossing the stile over the plantation fencing as the track becomes less clear. Cross the ladder stile in the stone wall ahead and continue up the faint grassy track, which later converges with the stone wall to the right as the track reduces to a path. Cross another stile, where the track is enclosed briefly between a wall and fence, and follow the wall to a clearer track.

   Note a commemorative plaque in the wall recording the loss of the 20 crew of a Flying Fortress on 8 June 1945.

4. Bear left along the fairly level stony track for about half a mile. Pass through the gate on the crest of the hill and carry on down the major track bending right then left. Follow this winding track through a gate, past the standing stone on the hillock to the left, and on through another gate. Converge with and join a metalled track soon passing through another gate. Turn left at a junction, signposted to Cregennan Lakes, past another standing stone.

   The twin lakes owned by the National Trust are beautifully situated in the shadow of Cadair Idris.

5. Immediately after passing a copse of conifers on the bank of the larger lake turn left at a finger post to follow a faint grassy track. Shortly after this track deteriorates to a path climb a substantial stone stile and follow the wall to the right. Go through the gate in the far right-hand corner of the field down a track, initially winding, then straight through several fields. Turn left at a junction of tracks as the Barmouth Estuary comes into view below.

6. Follow the level track ahead through a gate then bending left. Bear right away from the track, to cross the stone clapper bridge over the river and turn right. After 10 metres bear right over a ladder stile and follow the riverside path down the gorge. Go straight on at a junction of paths above a track and then bear left

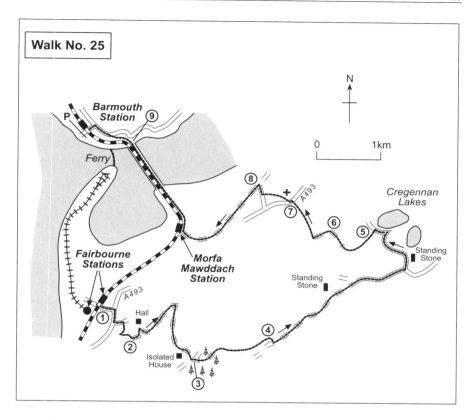

Walk No. 25

down the track. Where the track bends left through a barbed wire fence continue the descent along the obvious gorge path.

7. Emerge onto the A493 opposite Arthog church and turn left briefly. Turn right through the kissing gate and walk alongside the churchyard wall to an embankment. Follow the embankment to a lane and turn right.

> This is the Mawddach Trail, which takes its name from the beautiful estuary. The railway between Barmouth Junction (now Morfa Mawddach) and Dolgellau closed in 1965 after exactly 100 years. This popular trail is open to both cyclists and walkers.

8. Turn left along the disused railway line for about a mile and bear right across the road junction along the track signposted

Mawddach Trail. Bear right alongside the Cambrian Coast Line over the railway bridge into Barmouth.

This bridge was constructed in 1866 largely on timber trestles and was closed in 1980 for a period, the timber piles having been weakened by an attack of marine worm. The Barmouth end originally incorporated a swing bridge to allow large vessels to pass up the estuary.

9. Turn left to the harbour and town centre.

Walk 26: Talycafn to Llanfairfechan

Chester to Holyhead and Conwy Valley Lines

Starting point: Car parking in front of Llanfairfechan Station

Distance: 11 miles (17.7 kilometres)

Height gain: 1480 feet (450 metres)

Relevant maps: Explorer OL17 (Snowdon & Conwy Valley) Landranger 115 (Snowdon)

Facilities: Toilets a few hundred metres from Llanfairfechan Station, and in Llandudno Junction Station. Inn *en route* in Rowen and other facilities in Llanfairfechan.

Terrain: Good tracks interspersed by quiet country lanes and field paths. The indirect route to Rowen via Caerhun minimises the climbing, though there is a steep climb for the first half-mile out of Rowen. The next mile is a more gradual climb. Fairly clear route.

Take the train from Llanfairfechan to Talycafn (a request stop) changing at Llandudno Junction. This facilitates a walk along a historic track and passes many features of historical interest – Roman fort, ancient church, megalithic burial chamber, stone circle, and standing stones.

1. Turn right out of the station over the line and the River Conwy. Pass a small housing development and turn left down a track, later bearing right through a farmyard. Still in the farmyard, fork right as indicated around a large modern barn. Go through two field gates and walk along the bottom margin of a field. Cross the ladder stile in the corner of the field and follow the clear path through woodland. Leave the woods by way of a stile and go straight on across a field. Cross a ladder stile and walk straight on to join the stony track leading to Caerhun church.

    The Welsh placename refers to the 6th-century warrior prince, Rhun. St Mary's Church dates from the 13th century and is built on the site of a small Roman fort, Canovium. The latter was on the

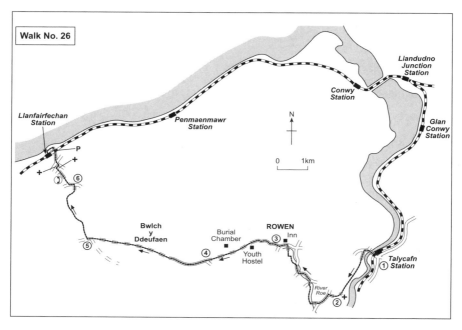

Roman road between Deva (Chester) and Segontium (Caernarfon)
and was also the end of Sarn Helen, the road which linked forts to
the south such as Tomen y mur (passed in the course of another
walk in this book). There is an information board in the lichgate
porch providing further information.

2. Carry on up the track to the road and turn left past the cemetery.
    Shortly after passing a lay-by turn right up a farm track. Cross a
    stream and turn right over a ladder stile and follow the stream
    climbing another three ladder stiles. Bear left to cross the ladder
    stile by a finger post near the far top corner of a field and turn
    right down a lane. Cross a gorge and turn left at a T-junction. Just
    before this lane crosses the river for the second time go through
    the kissing gate on the left. Follow the river and cross a ladder
    stile. Turn left alongside the fence, past a marker post, to the
    gateway by a small abandoned farmstead. Turn right along the
    enclosed track over a footbridge and turn left up the lane past
    the village inn of Rowen.

This lane, which deteriorates to a track, out of Rowen is the Roman road between Canovium and Segontium. It follows a track of prehistoric origin as evidenced by the standing stones, circle and burial chambers which litter the route.

3. Fork right at a junction of lanes climbing steeply for about a half-mile to the youth hostel where the lane deteriorates to a track. Follow the track for a good mile climbing more gradually.

In the course of this climb don't forget to look back at the marvellous views over the Conwy Valley and watch out for standing stones and burial sites. The most notable and easily found example is the megalithic burial chamber Maen-y-Bardd (The Bard's Stone), with its capstone still in place. Looking south at this point, the Iron Age hillfort of Pen-y-Gaer is on the peak with the jagged profile. Likewise, this burial site would have been visible from the fort.

The Bard's Stone Burial Chamber and guardian!

4. Bear right along a fairly level lane for another mile noting the small stone circle in a field to the left as the lane comes to an end. Carry on along the track ahead, over the pass of Bwlch y Ddeufaen, and between the two massive standing stones after

which the pass is named. Follow this track for another mile fording a stream at about the half-way point.

5. Turn right at a junction of tracks, indicated by a large finger post, to join the North Wales Path. Carry on down the major track through two junctions as indicated by marker posts. Pass between a stone wall and hill, soon diverging from the wall, still walking downhill. Go straight on where tracks fork – rather than going left towards the stone wall. Cross another track, after which the track bends right. Go through the kissing gate in the wall ahead and continue the increasingly steep descent down the obvious path, going straight on at a junction of paths. Nearing Llanfairfechan bear left over a ladder stile and follow an enclosed path. At the end of this enclosed section climb another ladder stile and bear left to a kissing gate.

6. Turn left along a lane leaving the North Wales Path and fork right at a junction. Go straight on at the next junction after which the lane narrows to a path. Pass alongside a golf course and then fork left between houses to a phone box. Turn right down the winding major road, as indicated by the road markings at several junctions. Bear right across a T-junction to go through the kissing gate at the side of an inn and down an enclosed path. Cross a footbridge over the river and turn left at the T-junction. Cross the road junction at traffic lights and go straight on to pass under the A55 and railway line. Turn left to go back to the station car park.

Walk 27: Dduallt to Tan-y-Bwlch via Tomen-y-mur

Ffestiniog Railway

Starting point: Tan-y-Bwlch Station car park, station signposted off A487 by the Oakeley Arms.

Distance: 11 miles (17.7 kilometres)

Height gain: 1450 feet (450 metres)

Relevant maps: Explorer OL18 (Harlech, Porthmadog and Bala), Landranger 124 (Dolgellau)

Facilities: Car parking, café and toilets at Tan-y-Bwlch. Refreshments *en route* in Maentwrog and Oakeley Arms.

Terrain: Tracks, paths and country lanes with some soft ground likely. Undulating ground with some energetic climbs and steep descents. Route finding is complex in the first two miles.

Local information: Nearby Plas Tan y Bwlch, now the Park residential study centre, belonged to the Oakeley family, then owners of the Blaenau Ffestiniog slate quarries. This walk passes through a renowned beauty spot, Ceunant Cynfal, and by the site of a Roman fort, Tomen-y-mur.

Take the train from Tan-y-Bwlch to Dduallt Halt, being sure to advise the guard of your destination.

> *This is the site of the only railway spiral in Britain. It was built by volunteers to divert the line of the preserved railway to pass along the upper side of the Tan-y-Grisiau Reservoir.*

1. Walk up to the top end of Dduallt Halt and go straight on along the original track bed, signposted to Rhyd y Sarn, and cross the ladder stile to the right. Follow the faint track alongside the old line down to a junction of tracks and turn right. Descend increasingly steeply and just before reaching a gate bear left along the less obvious track. Cross the ladder stile in the wall to the right and walk on alongside this wall. Cross the ladder stile ahead and descend through the dense conifer plantation along a

'Linda' passing the footpath sign starting to climb the loop above Dduallt Halt

broad path, then over rock outcrops. Bear left over a small stream leaving the plantation to descend a steep and rocky path, bending left. Cross the footbridge over the river and turn downstream. Go through the gate in the wall ahead and follow the obvious path through another gate and then along the track to the road.

2. Turn right along the A496 and just beyond the lay-by, turn sharply left up a narrow track. Where this track levels out turn right over a stile and climb away from the track. At the top of the field go through the gap in the wall and bear left into the valley. Turn right by a marker post along the valley for 50 metres then turn left through a kissing gate to climb steeply up an enclosed path to the B4391.

3. Turn right down the road and then cross the stile on the left, opposite a driveway. Walk up between the fence and wall then on alongside the wall to the right. Bear left over the dilapidated wall ahead and go through the handgate at the far end of the field. A few metres further on cross a ladder stile and follow the

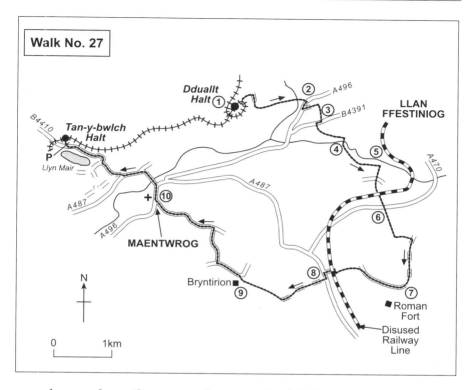

Walk No. 27

clear path up the gorge, Ceunant Cynfal, later crossing another ladder stile. Cross the stile by the gate ahead and turn right steeply downhill. Climb another stile and go down steps to cross the footbridge over the river and then climb steps to a junction of paths.

4. Turn left up the gorge along a well-worn path. Cross two stiles fairly close together where the path levels off. Bear left on reaching a field-gate, cross a stile, go through a handgate and then cross a stile above the next footbridge over the gorge.

    Detour a short distance over this bridge to see the principal waterfall, or walk further up the gorge to see a superb railway viaduct spanning the gorge and other waterfalls where this beautiful gorge is most accessible.

5. Turn right and climb up a partly paved path out of the gorge,

cross a stile and carry on alongside the wall to the left. Bear right across a lane up a farm track and turn left alongside a fence before reaching Cynfal Fawr. Go straight on under the railway line and up an enclosed path. Walk straight on over a field and turn right then left over the A496.

6. Walk up the hill, past a pylon and towards the finger post on the skyline. Cross the adjacent ladder stile and bear left to, but not over, the next ladder stile where a fingerpost indicates a junction of paths. Turn left by a fence to the right and then turn right at the corner of a conifer plantation along a surfaced track. Follow the track bending sharply right and over a cattle grid.

> *To the left is the site of the Roman fort, Tomen-y-mur, of which the ground-works are now barely discernible. The fort was 500ft by 350ft; it was built in AD78 and was similar in size to Canovium to the north in the Conwy Valley, to which it was connected by Sarn Helen. Sections of the road are still evident particularly near Dolwyddelan. The site also included a small amphitheatre. After the Romans abandoned the site about AD 130 it was adapted as home of the Welsh Princes of the Ardudwy. At some stage, parts of the fortifications were used to create Tomen-y-mur (mound on the wall), which is possibly a Norman motte.*

7. After about a half-mile turn left over a stile between a finger post and field gate, and follow the fence to the left for 50 metres. Turn right as indicated by a marker post and pass further marker posts, gradually converging with the bottom fence. Cross the stile in the bottom corner of the field and join a track to a barn. Turn left on the far side of the barn down a field and turn right along the bottom edge. Go through the gate in the corner to follow the track over the disused railway line to the road.

> *This is the same line as is spanned by the viaduct over the Ceunant Cynfal and was maintained as a transport link to Trawsfynydd power station – the only nuclear power station that was built inland. It opened in 1965 and closed in 1993.*

8. Turn left up the road and then turn right down the track opposite to a chapel. Go down this winding track to the right of a farm

and eventually reach a junction of tracks near to a pylon. Turn right along an improved track and, at the end of it, bear right up another track.

9.   Turn left down a lane by Bryntirion, fork right after a half-mile and turn left at a junction of lanes after a further half-mile, to descend into Maentwrog.

> *'Maen' means 'special stone', hence 'Maentwrog' refers to the stone of Twrog, a four-foot high monolith of uncertain origin by the belfry door of the church. It may be a prehistoric standing stone or ancient memorial stone.*

10. Bear right through the village and turn left along the A487. Turn right by the Oakeley Arms up the lane* and alongside Llyn Mair. Cross the footbridge at the far end of the car park and climb the stepped path to the station.

---

*   Alternatively, turn left opposite the Oakeley Arms up the driveway to Plas Tan y Bwlch. After crossing a stream turn right up a track through mature woodland, and later alongside the stream. Turn right at a junction of tracks to pass between two lakes, then turn left along the road by Llyn Mair. Cross the footbridge at the far end of the car park and climb the stepped path to the station. This permissive route is more attractive and safer than the road.

Walk 28: Pontsticill to Pant

Brecon Mountain Railway

Starting point: The terminus of the railway at Pant on the north side of Merthyr Tydfil. The railway is well signposted from the A470 and A465 which pass through the town. There is a large car park at the station.

Distance: 4 miles (6.4 kilometres)

Height gain: 260 feet (80 metres)

Relevant maps: Explorer OL12 (Brecon Beacons National Park, West & Central Areas) Landranger 160 (Brecon Beacons)

Facilities: Café and toilets at Pant station. Inns *en route* in the villages of Pontsticill and Pontsarn. Other facilities in Merthyr Tydfil.

Terrain: Field paths, track and quiet country lanes. Gently undulating ground, route-finding to Vaynor church is complex.

Local information: It is difficult to imagine now that Merthyr Tydfil was, following the Industrial Revolution, the largest settlement in Wales. The availability of coal, iron, limestone and water resulted in the establishment of ironworks and attracted a large workforce, and early technological advances such as canals, and railways. The decline started in the 1880s and has continued remorselessly. The museum and art gallery are housed in the neo-Gothic Cyfarthfa Castle, which was built in 1825 by the owner of the Cyfarthfa Ironworks. Ynysfach Engine House, part of the same ironworks, tells the story of ironmaking.

Pant Station is 340 metres above sea level! At the time of writing the track is only 3.5 miles long, but further extensions are planned to create a 5.5 mile length of line to the top end of the Torpantau Tunnel overlooking Glyn Collwn. This could open up opportunities for more ambitious linear walks. Take the train to Pontsticill, which will take about 30 minutes, as the train only stops on the return journey.

1. Go down the track at the end of the platform and along the lane ahead. Follow the major road over the dam of the reservoir and follow the road left then winding towards the village of

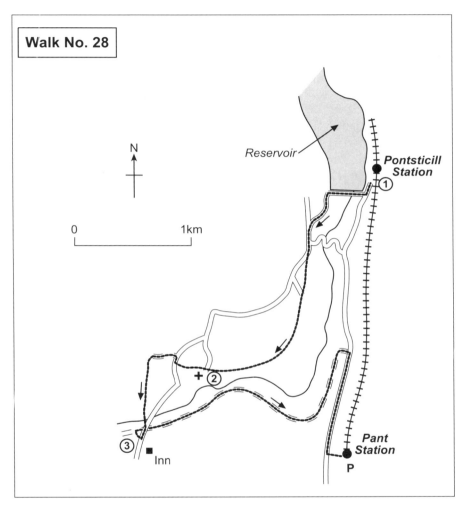

Walk No. 28

Pontsticill. Bear left at the road junction to pass The Red Cow Inn and, after 100 metres, bear left down the track to the right of Dolgaer Houses. At the end of this track bear right up an enclosed path to a lane and turn left. After 50 metres bear right at a finger post and go through the kissing gate ahead. Follow the initially clear level path then bear right, past a post carrying overhead cables, to go through another kissing gate in the fence ahead. Walk straight on to cross the stile in the far bottom corner of the field and turn left down a farm track. Go through a gate into the farmyard and immediately bear right to cross the stile at the end of the stone wall. Bear left along the field margin and go through the gate ahead. Pass through another gate to the left and turn right to descend by the hedge to the right. Go through the gate ahead and bear left to cross the stile in the stone wall. Bear right alongside the fence to the right and cross the stile by a gate in this fence to continue in the same direction. Cross yet another stile to join an enclosed path and then straight on by a fence to the right. Climb the stile in the far top corner of the field and follow the fence on the left to emerge at the end of a lane between Vaynor Church and a large house.

> *Until recently this house was the old Church Tavern, dating from the 13th century, though the present building is 17th century. The church, built of traditional materials in a curiously modern style, dates from 1870. This replaced the old church, passed very shortly, which dates from 1295. The earliest church to have ben built on the site dates from the 9th century.*

2. Turn left down the track, soon passing the remains of the old church, and cross a footbridge. Fork right up the bank then bear right alongside a fence to a lane. Turn right past the Italianate house and then turn left up a farm track signposted to Pontsarn Viaduct. Turn left along the bottom of the farmyard to cross a stile in the far bottom corner and join an enclosed path. At the end of this path cross the bridge and turn right opposite the inn, as signposted, down to the disused railway track.

> *This was the site of a station on the old Brecon and Merthyr Tydfil Line and the inn was originally the stationmaster's house. The nearby Pontsarn Viaduct, 450 feet long and over 90 feet high, was completed in 1866. The line was constructed mainly to carry coal and lime, but the beautiful valley below Pontsarn Station was a popular day trip destination in Victorian times.*

3. Turn right up the old trackbed over the viaduct. After following this old railway line for about a mile turn sharply right up the lane to Pant Station.

Checking the train before departure from Pant

Walk 29: Nantyronen to Aberystwyth via Capel Bangor

Vale of Rheidol Railway

Starting point: Vale of Rheidol Railway car park near to the station in the centre of Aberystwyth alongside the mainline station. *This car park is locked 30 minutes after the return of the last train,* but there are other car parks nearby. It is very easy to shorten this walk to 5 miles by starting the walk from Capel Bangor Halt (advise the guard if wishing to alight at this halt). *If you want to do this, please follow the instructions from the start of the third paragraph.*

Distance: 7.5 miles (12.1 kilometres) or 5 miles (8 kilometres)

Height gain: 200 feet (60 metres). Negligible on the shorter walk.

Relevant maps: Explorer 213 (Aberystwyth & Cwm Rheidol) Landranger 135 (Aberystwyth & Machynlleth)

Facilities: Full range in Aberystwyth

Terrain: Mainly tracks, improved paths and quiet country lanes and hence generally firm ground. Route finding generally easy.

Local information: Aberystwyth was a popular Victorian seaside resort, which continues to thrive as a university town and shopping centre for the sparsely populated area of central Wales. The Cliff Railway built in 1896 climbs Constitution Hill, a good viewpoint aided by the Camera Obscura. The huge 13th-century St Padarn's Church on the edge of town in the ancient hamlet of Llanbadarn Fawr hints at its importance in medieval times. The church contains two Celtic crosses which are 10th century or earlier. Aberystwyth is also home to the National Library of Wales.

Take the train and alight at the halt at Nantyronen having fore-warned the guard. The train will almost certainly stop there, travelling up the valley, to take on water. There are no parking facilities at the halts between Aberystwyth and Devil's Bridge, which limits opportunities for circular walks from this line, but there is some good walking at the top end of the line around Devil's Bridge.

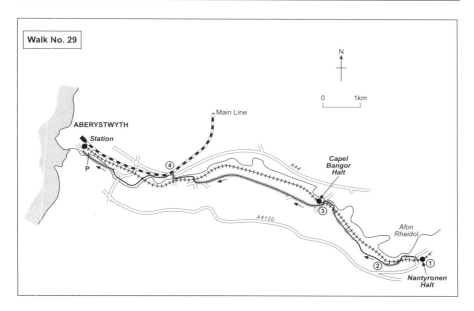

1. Walk away from the water tower, go through the handgate and turn right down the lane. Where the lane bends to the right turn left along the stony track. After about a half-mile cross the railway line and soon, where the track bends left between farm buildings, turn right through a field gate along a faint path parallel to the railway (do not go through the nearby gate onto the railway line).

2. Go through a belt of trees along the increasingly clear path. Follow the path uphill converging with a fence to the right. Go through the handgate in this fence and ford a stream. Carry on climbing through woodland and, at a clear waymarked junction of paths, turn right descending and eventually walking alongside the railway track. Go straight on past a level crossing where the path develops into a track with the railway still to the right. Pass another level crossing, where there are riding stables on the other side of the railway and the track is surfaced. Follow the track subsequently crossing the line, and then walking between the railway and the River Rheidol. On reaching a lane by Capel Bangor Halt turn left, again crossing the line.

'Prince of Wales' taking on water at Nantyronen before completing the climb to Devil's Bridge

3.   At the junction of lanes go straight on signposted Llanbadarn. Fork right at the next junction of lanes after about a half-mile to the end of this lane about a mile further on. At the junction with a major road turn right away from both roads and again cross the line to follow the improved track beside the railway. At the end of this track turn right across the bridge over the River Rheidol.

4.   Turn left at the T-junction and pass under the railway bridge. Turn left down a waymarked stepped path opposite terraced bungalows and cross the stile at the bottom of the enclosed path. Go straight on with a fence to the left and cross the main line railway embankment by way of two stiles. Bear right at two successive junctions of paths and carry on to join the improved waterside path along an embankment. Cross the Vale of Rheidol railway line for the last time and follow the river around the edge of playing fields. Pass under a road and turn left along the obvious path, diverging gradually from the river, to the road and turn left along this road back to the car park.

Walk 30: Llanfair Caereinion to Welshpool via Castle Caereinion

Welshpool and Llanfair Light Railway

Starting point: Welshpool and Llanfair Light Railway Station car park *(gates locked at 5.30pm)* on the west side of Welshpool. The walk passes near to the station at Castle Caereinion creating the option of a shorter walk. The walk from Castle Caereinion to Welshpool is easy, being less than 4 miles in length with minimal height gain.

Distance: 10.5 miles (16.9 kilometres) or 4 miles (6.4 kilometres)

Height gain: 1100 feet (330 metres) or negligible.

Relevant maps: Explorer 215 (Newtown & Machynlleth) and 216 (Welshpool & Montgomery), Landranger 125 (Bala & Lake Vyrnwy, Berwyn) and 126 (Shrewsbury)

Facilities: Wide range of facilities in Welshpool, café and toilets at both stations, other facilities in Llanfair Caereinion. Inn at Castle Caereinion.

Terrain: Mostly tracks and quiet country lanes, generally firm and some fields. Three short climbs between Llanfair Caereinion and the village of Castle Caereinion followed by a gradual descent into Welshpool. Route finding generally straightforward except for the two miles through fields after leaving Castle Caereinion.

Local information: Welshpool is an attractive, thriving town with a good range of shops, interesting buildings and bisected by the Montgomery Canal which is gradually being reopened and reconnected to the Llangollen Canal. Powysland Museum is in an old warehouse on the canal wharf. The magnificent Powis Castle is a mile out of town.

Take the train from Welshpool to Llanfair Caereinion or Castle Caereinion.

1.   Turn left out of the station and cross the footbridge over the river signposted to the town centre. At the end of the enclosed path bear left out of the cul-de-sac and turn right along the road. At the end of Wesley Street, at the T-junction, turn left up the major

'The Earl', at the terminus in Welshpool

road and climb out of the town. Turn left along a waymarked path by the top fence of the recreation ground. Cross the stile ahead and turn uphill to cross another stile in the top left-hand corner of the field. Follow the obvious path between houses and bear left up an initially surfaced track. The surface deteriorates on passing a modern barn. Bear left along the side of a field where the track is less distinct. Walk on through field gates and several fields by the fence or hedge to the right and later between mature trees.

2. At the end of this track turn right along the lane and, after half a mile, turn left at a junction of lanes by Brynelen Farm. Turn right at the next junction (Cyfronydd Halt is about 100 metres ahead) initially climbing steeply as the surface deteriorates to a rough track which continues for about a mile. Turn sharply right at the next junction, where the surface improves, and descend to the B4385.

3. Turn left along the road for about 200 metres and bear right in

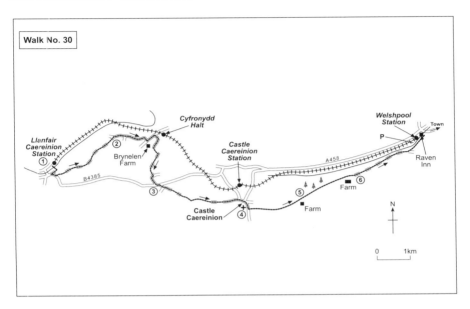

Walk No. 30

the hollow, then climbing up a lane which also soon deteriorates to a rough track. Follow the track winding across a field and ford a stream in a belt of woodland. Go through the gate at the end of the track and bear right alongside the fence. Pass through another gate ahead and go straight on across a field to the bottom corner of woodland. Go through the gate and bear left down a clear track, later surfaced, to Castle Caereinion. Bear left and then right along the main road through the village (the station is a short distance left down the main road).

The Victorian church is on a historic site where the castle would have originally been sited, and of which there is now no trace.

4.   Follow the main road winding through the village. 75 metres after passing Castle Chapel on the outskirts of the village turn left over the stile by a field gate. Cross the field diagonally to climb the stile in the opposite corner and walk on alongside the hedge to the right. Cross the stile in this hedge and carry on alongside the ditch to the right. Cross a footbridge/stile combination and bear right soon walking alongside a hedge to the right. Cross another stile in this hedge under an oak tree. Bear

right across the next field and follow the hedge opposite as it bends left. Cross the stile by the gate in the corner of the field and walk along the bottom margin of more fields. Eventually join a stony track towards a farm. As the track bends to the right of the farm, go straight on as indicated by a marker post to pass to the left of the farm.

5.   Climb a stile when abreast of the farm and walk on to cross the farm track below by way of two stiles. Bear left up the valley through a long field to cross the stile at the bottom corner of woodland. Bear right, diverging from the woodland, to the field gate in view ahead. Cross the stile by this gate and bear left to the far bottom corner of the field. Cross a stile and bear right to cross another stile, then bear left across the front of a cattle shed. Cross the stile in the far bottom corner of the field and pass along the bottom margin of the next field. Climb a stile, awkwardly placed by a ditch, and walk straight on through a field gate along the track winding between the buildings of a large farm.

6.   Carry on down this track, later metalled, for about a mile. At the end of the improved surface where the track bends sharply left, go straight on over a stile up a minor track. After 150 metres bear left at a marker post to gradually descend and cross the stile at the far bottom end of the field. Follow the stream down the valley and cross further stiles. On reaching the road on the outskirts of Welshpool, turn left past the Raven Inn to the station car park.

Also of interest:

OFFA'S DYKE CIRCULAR WALKS: Northern Section
Ian Coulthard

Here are 25 challenging circular walks based on the Offa's Dyke National Trail from Prestatyn to Knighton. The walks range from 6 to 13 miles (3 to 7 hours), sampling the delights of some of the best hill walking in the country. Detailed but concise instructions include height gain, local facilities and summaries of terrain and ground conditions. *£6.95*

SNOWDONIA WALKS WITH CHILDREN
Nick Lambert

Snowdonia is known for for its mountain scenery, but there are many areas in the spectacular valleys that are ideal for families – either completely flat, or with gentle climbs. These 20, circular walks cover the whole of Snowdonia, taking in a wide variety of the National Park's scenery. Questions and answers along the way add to the fun! *£6.95*

BEST TEA SHOP WALKS IN SNOWDONIA
Dorothy Hamilton

Forget hard days in the mountains – enjoy Snowdonia at a leisurely pace and round it off with a yummy Welsh tea! Walks from 3½ to 8 miles, for all ages and experience. Climb Conwy mountain, explore Gwydr Forest, or walk in the Lledr and Ffestiniog valleys. *£6.95*

BEST TEA SHOP WALKS IN THE CLWYDIAN HILLS AND WELSH BORDERLANDS
Dorothy Hamilton

25 family walks from 3 to 10 miles through the Clwydian Hills. The routes take you to the spectacular Eglwyseg escarpment, and splendid sections of the Offa's Dyke path. Clear directions, sketch maps, photographs and notes on local history and wildlife are included. *£6.95*

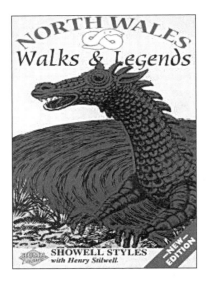

BEST TEA SHOP WALKS IN LLEYN & ANGLESEY
Dorothy Hamilton
Explore magnificent cliff scenery with dramatic views of offshore islands, visit picturesque coastal hamlets and remote valleys or walk beside rushing rivers. Each route includes a 'tea shop stop' personally recommended by the author, and to feed your mind there are notes on local history and wildlife. £6.95

NORTH WALES WALKS AND LEGENDS
Showell Styles with Henry Stilwell
Discover new places in this beautiful landscape, and enjoy the old stories that belong here. With a selection of 18 walks you could be in for a surprise! Will it be fairies, giants, heroes or beasts? Route maps and directions accompany each walk and there are beautifully intricate line drawings throughout. £6.95

NORTH WALES WALKING ON THE LEVEL
Norman Buckley
Circular walks for those who enjoy walking in fine surroundings, without significant ascents. Descriptions of towns and villages, landscape and interesting features are included. The author advises on whether any ascent is steep and concentrated, or is gradual and divided into several parts. £6.95

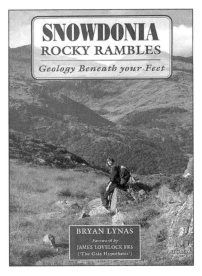

SNOWDONIA ROCKY RAMBLES: Geology Beneath your Feet
Bryan Lynas
This is much more than a book of mountain walks. Each of the ten routes is a voyage of discovery and a journey through time, with insights into the geology, wildlife and history of these splendid peaks. Highly detailed maps, excellent diagrams and annotated photographs help to explain the trickiest points even to non-scientists. £9.95

All of our books are available through booksellers. In case of difficulty, or for a free catalogue, please contact: **SIGMA LEISURE, 5 ALTON ROAD, WILMSLOW, CHESHIRE SK9 6AR.**
Phone/Fax: 01625-531035   E-mail: info@sigmapress.co.uk
Web site: http//www.sigmapress.co.uk